"In my 25 years as an entrepreneur, there has l of business decisions. *Dare to Care* boldly disrup and economics that integrates heart and mind, l economic facts with lyrical poetry. It highlights profits which employ Care-First vs. Money-First as a long overdue pathway to true sustainability for all people of the world."—**Leslie Danziger, Co-founder and former Chairman of Solaria Corporation, USA**

"If you Dare to Care, then Louis Böhtlingk's transformative book will open your mind. Money is no longer the free-market evil. It is now a force for good and the foundation of a practical solution which transcends capitalism and enables society to realize its highest purpose—a loving and co-operative harmony. Read this book and find the pathway we all seek through thinking differently about only one thing—money."— **Pippa Bartolotti, Founder of COEXIST, United Kingdom**

"Louis Böhtlingk has given us a clear way to create a renewed sense of how to assess the tools we have and our needs. The poetry of *Dare to Care* is a personal policy that should become the basis of a newly defined economic policy for all. How do we turn it into a new course book for candidates seeking Economic PhD degrees?"— **Michaela Walsh, President/Founder of Women's World Banking, USA**

"In his well-thought and heart-centered book, *Dare to Care*, Louis Böhtlingk defines the Garden state on Earth, as a 'place of happiness and joy, togetherness and peace, where all are well, fed, housed, educated and healthy and Nature has been brought back to its natural abundance with its eco-systems restored.' I could not agree more. If all of today's children and their families were educated and empowered within a 'Care-First' paradigm, lovingly integrated into Forest Garden Community School programs all over the world, many of the unsustainable behaviors associated with today's global crisis would be eliminated in a generation."—**Donna L. Goodman, Founder/ Director, Earth Child Institute, USA**

"A profound reminder that once money is used for loving care of the planet and its people, its transformative power creates limitless possibilities for peace, abundance, joy, and freedom for all. Deep transformative change of our financial system is long overdue. Now is the time to energize our money flows with the gift of loving care as our new currency of exchange. From now onwards, let us Dare to Care and resolve to co-create a whole new way of life by 2025."—**Steven Lovink, Founder of Power of One and Planet2025 Network, USA**

"We need to stop being scared of ideas developed earlier than last year! Let's admit that the dilemmas faced today were apparent decades ago and that brilliant minds saw the challenges, predicted the wrong turns and offered solutions. That we globally faltered, were blind to what our visionaries saw, declined to learn from them, is a failure we must accept and learn from. *Dare to Care* is so well researched and brilliantly hopeful that it bridges the decades and insists we learn from our hearts and move forward, knowing giants have lead the way. We need not falter again."—**Rosalinda Sanquiche, Executive Director of Ethical Markets Media, USA**

"Like Daedalus, we appear to be trapped in a financial labyrinth of our own making. Having been out of step with orthodoxy all my life, often not understanding why, my heart gladdens in finding a fellow dance partner who can show me new steps. Spirit and heart, so long absent in our financial dealings with each other, are finally here at the leading edge of business thinking. We have not a moment to lose."—**Quentin Cowen, profession chef, United Kingdom**

"*Dare to Care* contains the seed thoughts for our time. By sharing our abundance, we multiply, create and move forward. This book inspires a deep transformation of the human race: from control to sharing, from possessing things to using them, from having to being . . . *Dare to Care* unites all cultures in one language. Becoming one world where we share our resources and reunite our cultures will naturally transform the old structures and rationale. Thank you, dear author, for bringing the news at the right moment."—**Nik Laansma, author and coach, the Netherlands**

"If you have perhaps known for a long time that the global financial systems that rule our world are deeply flawed, but have not quite articulated in your own mind exactly what is wrong with them, let alone what can you do in your own life to put them right, then this book is for you. Louis Bohtlingk develops these concepts further, seeking 'the Essence of the Essence': Love replacing Fear as the fundamental driver behind the way we think about, use, spend, save, invest, hoard, and waste money. Louis shows through countless examples how this has the capacity to maximize the common good and, in so doing, turn the entire global economic system on its head and give us a world of abundance and contentment, now and for generations to come."—**Rosalinda Copisarow, Managing Director of Oikocredit, the Netherlands**

"In the 20th century, many change agents were engaged in perhaps fruitless debates about whether change was personal or social, i.e whether it had to target the self or social structures first. 'Change yourself and society will change' vs. 'change society, and people will change.' Fortunately today, more and more integral change approaches are emerging where those efforts are combined. In this book, this effort is applied to our economic and financial system, and to the role of money in particular. While it analyzes what's wrong structurally, Louis Bohtlingk does not hesitate to tackle the psychological and spiritual attitudes that stand in the way of a true social and monetary transformation. The message needs to be heard; change yourself and change society, simultaneously."—**Michael Bauwens, Founder of the P2P Foundation, Thailand**

"*Dare to Care* is truly a new paradigm book, accurately defining an urgently necessary yet supremely appealing new way of being in relationship with money for this new millennium. It is an essential guide for the integration of the spiritual and material within us toward our ultimate evolution in these tumultuous and transformative times. Louis Bohtlingk has written an important book that dares and profoundly inspires us to consistently care from a place of universal and unconditional love."—**Candice Powers, M.A., numerologist/universalist, neurofeedback therapist, USA**

"*Dare to Care* challenges us to re-evaluate our basic relationship with money and our current economic system. A "Care First World" is one where money serves the well being of people and the Earth, with an economic system based on love, caring, and sharing. *Dare to Care* sets out a stimulating challenge for all of us to look at our personal and organizational economic values. Well done!"—**John Zwerver, President of Global Family, USA**

DARE TO CARE

Dear Henry and Marion,
With many blessings
Louis C.F Böhtlingk

www. carefirstworld. com / blog

DARE TO CARE

A LOVE-BASED FOUNDATION FOR MONEY AND FINANCE

LOUIS BÖHTLINGK

WITH ERNIE ROBSON

FOREWORD BY HAZEL HENDERSON

COSIMO BOOKS

NEW YORK

Cosimo aims to publish books that inspire, inform, and engage readers worldwide. We use innovative print-on-demand technology that enables books to be printed based on specific customer needs. This approach eliminates an artificial scarcity of publications and allows us to distribute books in the most efficient and environmentally sustainable manner. Cosimo also works with printers and paper manufacturers who practice and encourage sustainable forest management, using paper that has been certified by the FSC, SFI, and PEFC whenever possible.

Ordering Information:
Cosimo publications are available at online bookstores. They may also be purchased for educational, business, or promotional use:
Bulk orders: Special discounts are available on bulk orders for reading groups, organizations, businesses, and others.
Custom-label orders: We offer selected books with your customized cover or logo of choice.

For more information, contact us at:

Cosimo, Inc.
P.O. Box 416, Old Chelsea Station
New York, NY 10011

info@cosimobooks.com

or visit us at:
www.cosimobooks.com

TABLE OF CONTENTS

PART THREE: A CARE-FIRST WORLD

DARE TO CARE
a Love-Based Foundation for Money and Finance

The relationship between money and care is profound.
When we dare to let care lead the way in all financial and economic processes
and money serves caring,
a completely fresh, vibrant, and transformational foundation for finance
and for our economies emerges.
This foundation will bless us for generations to come
and will fully sustain all we are and our beautiful Earth.

We call it the magic of care-first over money-first,
where money is being used in service
to our values and the well-being of people and the Earth,
rather than at their expense.
The new foundation we have created is love-based, because care is love in action.
This foundation and our cooperation with each other
will set a new tone for the future of our economies and finance.

As we truly meet and deeply listen,
letting our hearts and minds speak
to the issues at hand,
a place opens up among us
that serves us all!

This common ground is where
our global financial commons resides.
It is a shared space in which we can express
our concerns and apply our resolutions
toward addressing the state of our financial world and of our economies.

The sun can shine again upon all we re-create
based on the voice of our heart and its intelligence,
be it our monetary system,
the functioning of our financial institutions,
or transforming our lives with money, survival, and work.

As we slowly but steadily make this breakthrough
by keeping the best of what we've created so far
and rebuilding what is malfunctioning,
we will create what our hearts know to be true:
a world where love reigns over each of us and over our cultures.

Our children need us to relate, to give and receive,
as they so often naturally do themselves.
We deeply need what our sharing heart feels and brings to us.
That innocence is real.
It is not something to lose as we grow up!

FOREWORD

My first encounter with Louis Böhtlingk was in late 2010, in an hour-long phone conversation. We explored each other's mission and goals for transforming finance and for money-creation, and our shared belief that the way economies are structured functions to distort human behavior and inhibit our natural impulses toward trust, bonding, sharing, and cooperation.

At that time, Louis had not yet encountered my life's work of researching and developing the concept of the Love Economy and creating new metrics beyond economics to measure the unpaid sectors and overall quality of life. As I explained my passion, based on what I had learned from my mother, Louis and I shared an epiphany. Louis invited me to co-author a book with him, as we compared our life experiences and what he and his wife Sandra have discovered during their workshops on "Meeting the Mystery of Money." I saw the immense value of their many years of empirical research about how dysfunctional economic structures and theories can stunt human development, upset relationships, cause unnecessary conflicts, warp lives, and foreclose on opportunities for our children to create more loving, harmonious societies.

Louis and Sandra's work had been recommended to me by my two dear long-time friends, John Steiner and Steve Schueth, and this convinced me to help Louis with this book. I urged Louis to be the author of this book, and I acceded to his plan to visit with me for the month of November 2010 for daily consultations in drafting it. In this way, we sought to blend our experience with what was wrong with economics (the current dysfunctional social structures and beliefs based on false theories); to elucidate the "Love Economies" that are unnoticed by economic statistics; and to lay out the rich menu of deeper, more cohesive ways of being and behaving within our human behavioral repertoire.

I have always known that each human being is a wondrous package of potential, shaped by evolution, nature, and nurture for good; the glass is at least half full. As Louis and I sat in my living room each day, we explored the many social forces influencing human behavior. I had also agreed to write this Foreword, and I enjoyed introducing Louis to my own research and key books in my 5,000-volume library at Ethical Markets Media. This typical global Internet company, a strong PageRank 6 on Google[1] with more than 30,000 links, is based in the garage of the 100-year-old house I share with my spouse of 20 years, computer pioneer Alan F. Kay.[2]

One of my dearest friends and mentors, E. F. Schumacher, author of *Small Is Beautiful* and who wrote the Foreword to my first book, *Creating Alternative Futures: The End of Economics*, always told me that being a successful change agent meant choosing not to take credit or fame but to fly under the radar. I followed his advice and realized that to challenge the vanities, absurdities, and power of the economics profession, I would not need to grow an organization, but instead to become a strand of cultural DNA, a living, stable molecule of information that does not grow, but replicates itself. For years, my personal business card read "intellectual boutique for re-designing cultural DNA." I saw economics as a piece of malfunctioning source code deep in the hard drives of our institutions that colonized the minds of people—truly a dysfunctional strand of cultural DNA, replicating misinformation in our body politic, which needed teasing out and correcting. This effort brought me a sustainable income and livelihood over the past 40 years, writing and thinking and working as a lecturer for many organizations who heard my high-fidelity birdcall.

Since I published my first of several articles in the *Harvard Business Review* in 1968, I have circled our beautiful planet, speaking to groups in over 50 countries. All of them wanted to know what was wrong with economics and how I had moved toward systems thinking and multidisciplinary analyses of our dysfunctional, conflict-ridden societies that were at war with nature. I joined with groups of renegade scientists and futurists and served as a science policy wonk on advisory councils at the US Congress Office of Technology Assessment, the National Science Foundation, and the National Academy of Engineering, as well as with the

Calvert Group of socially responsible mutual funds in Washington, D.C. All these various organizations were trying to see beyond conventional economics, long before their disastrous effects on all our lives in the financial meltdowns in Latin America and Asia. The Wall Street collapse of 2007–2008 is still causing pain, hunger, and misery to millions of innocent victims around the world. Without deep reforms, we all are all risking another collapse.

Louis and I talked continuously about all these issues: confusing money with real wealth (healthy, knowledgeable humans and the vast ecological assets of Nature) and how this had led to error-prone money creation, the politics of economics and credit allocation, and their ultimate source in human ego drives for power and control. For many years, I had discussed these same issues in patriarchal societies with my long-time friends Riane Eisler and her spouse David Loye. David's many books influenced me as a futurist, and his later partnership with Riane has led to their collective and individual work through their Center for Partnership Studies. Louis and Sandra Böhtlingk had also observed the corrosive effects of patriarchal structures within the family, which were evident in their workshops.

Thus, I have special joy in writing this Foreword, since it brings together so many strands in my life, as well as strands of the lives of Louis and Sandra and those they touch. I am particularly thrilled that my Love Economy work can reach further, as can the Calvert-Henderson Quality of Life Indicators. We no longer need economists or any single discipline to measure national progress. We can use the multi-disciplinary systems, "dashboard" approach that the Calvert Group and I pioneered, allowing a single website to display 12 indicators that track national trends, including those not properly captured by gross domestic product (GDP) and money measures: health, education, environment, human rights, energy efficiency, re-creation (self-revitalization), and even infrastructure, which are also ignored in the GDP measurement.

That is why Ethical Markets Media has funded surveys on "Beyond GDP" with global polling firm Globescan, which confirm that, since the 2007 conference I co-organized in the European Parliament (*www.beyond-gdp.eu*), ordinary people in 12 countries widely understand the need for including all the indicators of quality of life in GDP. Correcting GDP by including all the forms of wealth beyond money, including well-educated populations, efficient infrastructure, and productive environments, could show that so-called "insolvent countries" in the Euro-zone are actually more prosperous and healthier than the financial markets and their bond vigilantes understand from their focus on GDP, as I wrote in "GDP: Grossly Distorted Picture" (*CSRWire,* January 23, 2011).

These and other sins of omission and faulty theories instead lead market players to buy credit default swaps, betting that these European countries will default—hoping for a killing. Similar economic models caused the financial collapse and now fuel current speculation in oil, food, and other commodities, causing hunger, hardship, and political uprisings. The "austerity" budgets and budget cuts in many countries, including the US, are part of the latest form of class warfare between Wall Street and Main Street. Main Street is losing, as economic fundamentalists force cuts on teachers, fire-fighters, and police; strip the rights of unions to collective bargaining, and jeopardize their pensions.

I deeply hope *Dare to Care* becomes a huge bestseller and can help to finally end the ideologies of economics and even its reformist hybrids: ecological economics, social economics, behavioral economics (all stolen from other disciplines and more scientific research), as I described in *The Politics of the Solar Age* in 1981. Economics has colonized public and private decision-making for too long, as conferees agreed at the November 2004 seminar, "What Next in Economics," which I co-sponsored in St. Augustine, Florida, at Ethical Markets Media with Sweden's Dag Hammarskjöld Foundation. I agree with Nassim Nicholas Taleb, author of *The Black Swan* (not the movie!), that economics is actually useless for decisions in our modern world and that business school curricula should be reformed or the schools should be shut down. While those statements may sound extreme, I believe they are part of a necessary challenge if we want to lead our lives based on what's for the benefit of all of humanity (which is what *Dare to Care* is fundamentally about).

I urge all readers to also read Ethical Markets' 2010 statement on Transforming Finance, which recognizes finance as a part of the global commons, and to join the over 80 world experts in signing it at *www. TransformingFinance.net.*

Lastly, I salute my fellow researchers of the Darwin Project (*www. thedarwinproject.com*), led by David Loye's book *Darwin's Lost Theory of Love* and other books by him and by Riane Eisler, which show how Charles Darwin's work was hijacked by Victorian elites in Britain to justify their social privilege as "the survival of the fittest." This poisoned phrase, as *The Economist* admitted in 2005, was coined not by Charles Darwin, but by Herbert Spencer, its editor, and had led to the narrow focus of the economics profession on competition, as I recounted in my book *Ethical Markets: Growing the Green Economy*. *The Economist* went on to admit that economics has ignored the other half of human behavior and societies: cooperation.

This is what my work, including my love economy research and Louis's *Dare to Care,* seek to bring to the light of day.

—*Hazel Henderson*
St. Augustine, Florida
April 2011

*D*are to Care is all about a change of heart. We can move from a money-first to a care-first attitude. This means we *use money in service to our values and the well-being of all people and living systems of the Earth and not at their expense.* We can resolve the financial and economic crises we are in and move towards a truly sustainable foundation for generations to come. We can do this by reestablishing the magic of the five simple human qualities of *caring, sharing, loving, giving, and receiving.* This will redeem the suffering in our financial and economic worlds caused by not listening to the language of our hearts.

We can apply this to our daily business practices, to paying our bills, to all our financial and economic activities, and to the laws and regulations of our countries and the world. Throughout this book, we will show that whenever we have been motivated by greed, fear, selfishness, possessiveness, and desire for power, we have only created pain and trouble in our financial and economic worlds. However, where caring, sharing, loving, giving, and receiving were applied, well-being was created every single time.

The transition we need to make is simple in concept; in practice, however, it is a huge task and requires a profound change of attitude. Because of our deeply ingrained conditioning through childhood and the selfish behavior so often promoted in our lives regarding money, we are not so familiar with the relationship between money and these five loving qualities. We have a long way to go. The great hope is that with our heart's intelligence, common sense, and willingness to cooperate, we can resolve the issues at hand.

My friend Steve Schueth suggested the title of this book to me: *Dare to Care.* He is president of the First Affirmative Financial Network in

Boulder, Colorado, and has assisted us in an advisory manner since 2002. He said in a testimonial in support of our work something so profound, yet so simple:

> Care first. It sounds so simple. Fortunately, some of the most profound and meaningful aspects of life are the simplest. Louis and Sandra have shone their light on a universal law that many of us knew to be there lurking behind the cloud of greed and fear that has developed over the centuries, and they have given it a name. A simple, elegant name. If everyone in the world used money with the intention of care-first, many, if not all, of the problems of the world would be eliminated in a generation. That is the dream. That is the possibility.

In 2001, two days before 9/11, at the Socially Responsible Investing (SRI) in the Rockies Conference in Tucson, Arizona, I said in the opening address, entitled "A Care-First World Vision,"

> When we live with the intention of care-first, we address the social, environmental, economical, and political issues in our life, community and world, without saying, "We cannot look at this because there is no money in the budget!" We make sure that we look at it, and once we know what needs doing, we manifest the flow of finance, resources, and events needed. I can see a real breakthrough of caring in the world. A process where money is serving the caring everywhere, because we become clear about the illusions of money-first and the power of care-first. Let's consider a care-first world vision. Can you see what happens when our conflicts around money resolve? When people lose their self-protectiveness and fear around money and are working together and supporting one another with it? Can you see this new dance, this new release, this new horizon?

To receive and share the gifts of the Earth and steward them properly provides our financial world and our economies with a strong and very healthy foundation. The whole financial and economic world is a part of this gift; nothing is exempt. Everything was given to us by creation. It all belongs to us and we need to allow ourselves to receive and share that gift, which we can also call our *global commons.* A global financial commons is also a part of this; we will look at this in more detail throughout this book.

I hope that *Dare to Care:*

1. Shows us that the way of the heart is fully possible and applicable in the field of economics and finance, and that it helps us to have a whole new perspective around money.
2. Instills in us a sense of gratitude for life's gifts, which can imbue our financial and economic thinking and which promotes sharing.
3. Instills in us the idea of a global financial commons as a new point of focus and stimulates us to look at how we can more equitably distribute our finances and resources.

I believe that *we* are that change and that it is happening through us. This change is an organic process, which began through the financial and economic collapse that is going on worldwide. As one thing dies, another comes to life; as the war with money ends, the peace with money can start.

Many subjects in *Dare to Care* can be categorized as "soft." The business and financial world is often described as "hard." However, I only look at what works and what doesn't work. It is my experience that these soft-heart-based concepts are very powerful and uplifting and can help to shape a new foundation. In the field of economics and finance, we need warmth, common sense, and, foremost, care. I say "dare to care," because caring is quite a step to take in the world of money. It takes courage because it is connected to overcoming our fears and conditioning. I invite you, as a reader, to travel with me on a journey through the land of money to see whether we can come to a place where we feel empowered and reassured by the notion that "Yes, we can resolve this situation together." This is possible when we dare to care, dare to share, dare to love, dare to give, and dare to receive.

INTRODUCTION

Dear Reader: I wish to share with you some of the wisdom and insight I have learned in the process of writing this book. Throughout this book, I will share some of the collective wisdom that has been shared with me and that has inspired me. The first comment is from John Steiner (networker, social activist, consultant, and philanthropist from Boulder, Colorado), who previewed the book:

> This is a remarkable book that, perhaps uniquely, brings together a range of information, vision, experience, possibilities, love, and caring about the kind of financial world a majority of earth's citizens would clearly want if they knew it was an option. It also courageously chronicles the experience, vision, and actualization of its author. It is a treasure trove.
>
> One suggestion to the reader: As we each have our own particular religious, spiritual, psychological, humanistic, personal approach to life and to the world, so does the author. Therefore, as you're reading through his experienced and heartfelt approach to demystifying money and draining the fear so many of us have around money (mostly about not having enough), while offering a plausible and historically relevant alternative, do provide yourself whatever metaphors and framework work for you. In other words, feel free to translate Louis' approach into your own. In fact, as you'll see, he is inviting such participation to reach ever larger audiences and actively engage you.

Another previewer, Ruth Turner of Charlottesville, Virginia, described the book as: "an excellent, eye-opening and inspiring resource for healing (transforming) self and society."

A number of people reviewed the book; it is clear that many experience the book in the way Ruth describes it.

We need a deeply personal transformation so that we can in turn transform our financial and economic lives in the direction we want to go. We also need to cooperate with each other at a local, national, and international level and transform our financial and economic systems and how they are being regulated, where needed.

In order for us to be able to make the changes proposed in this book, it is very important to understand that the inner world of our thoughts, feelings, emotions, etc., and our outer world of behaviors and actions are constantly interactive; we need to be aware of both. Without making the inner shift from fear to love, without working on ourselves, we can never come to the creation of a better world. However, when we do not deal with the form of our outer world, the way we all live together and have organized ourselves, and do not apply our inner changes to this, we will not make the progress we need.

Peter Blom, chief executive officer of Triodos Bank, says:

> Positive solutions also require authenticity—not in a vague introspective way, but in a meaningful sense that is linked to our actions. True innovation that makes a lasting sustainable difference will come from people who combine an inward and outward focus.[3]

To quote my dear friend and colleague Jon Freeman, from his latest book *Future Money: The Way We Survive Global Bankruptcy*[4]:

> Throughout, it has been stressed many times that the shift comes from within. The actions that Louis lists [see the Four Actions, Chapter 2] are foundational aspects of that internal impulse. Out of that impulse, we can individually and collectively take the steps which will deliver a sustainable form of economic life and a healthy version of money.[5]

MOVING FROM FEAR TO LOVE

Fear and love are two fundamental experiences of all human beings. From the force of fear come the emotions of greed, the desire for power, possessiveness, and selfishness. From the force of love come the emotions of sharing, caring, loving, giving, and receiving.

Love empowers us; fear disempowers us and disables us. Love gives us a sense of expansion; fear creates a sense of limitation. Love moves us forward; fear holds us back. Love creates a sense of abundance; fear, a sense of scarcity. Fear thinks we can't change; love knows we can.

I acknowledge that both are serving us; both play their rightful part and by moving through the experiences of fear and love, we learn our lessons and mature into seeing what a new and sustainable approach to finance and economics can look like. Through the balance of light and dark, we find the door. What goes on in our money system is symptomatic of that which plays itself out internally, deep inside of us all.

DARE TO CARE—A PLAN OF ACTION

This book is about wanting to create a platform to see how we can find clarity about maneuvering ourselves through the huge and profound economic and financial crisis we are in. It is about creating a platform to rebuild the monetary system, where needed, and to give our economies a truly sustainable foundation for generations to come. It is a platform for us all, whether we build the roads or clean the streets, take care of children at home or do volunteer work; whether we are artists, craftspeople, work in government, at a university, or in business; whether we act in the movies or are kings or queens. We're creating a platform for all of us to work together.

We are in a situation where whole economies and countries can fall. What do we need to do to create true stability, freedom, equality, and fairness?

In this book I will share a range of possibilities and inspirations received by me and others, and I will give many practical examples of their application to helping us think and feel together. Profound change starts with the premise that the answers we look for lie in our midst. Change starts with the realization that we need each other and need to share our communications, so that we can become clear about our direction. As individuals, we only know so much, but when we combine our efforts, we can come to the clarity we need. I can't stress strongly enough the importance of understanding the need to work together to find the answers!

It is through the magic of all of us coming together that we can make things work. We can create a powerful tapestry containing all the different colors held by us as global citizens, communities, and countries. Each individual, each group, each country is so unique.

I want to create a space for all our unheard voices. We each have our perceptions, visions and ideas of what we want our world to look like. Unfortunately, most of us feel helpless in relation to what governments decide or what big corporations do, and thus we become unclear about how we can help to create our world. *We want to create a shared space where we can all speak and be heard,* a space for us to see where we can take all that we are feeling and seeing and channel this into manifesting the world we want.

We invite all who are reading this book to share ideas, inspirations, and initiatives in relation to how you visualize the changes we need to make. We would love to hear about your situation, your community, your country. We want to hear what you think, see, and feel about the issues we raise in this book. Feel free to make proposals about how we can work together. Let your voice be heard! *We will create an online platform for this purpose, which will include input from experts. You can find more about its development on our website, www.CareFirstWorld.com.*

To help us all move forward together in making the shift toward an economy and financial world that we would like to see, we have opened up a space to work together and participate in *seven levels of transformation.* It starts with the possibility of working on ourselves and assisting each other with deep transformation. Then we can move to working in teams; then we connect and bring the teams together; and then we can turn that work into political action and promote necessary changes in legislation and regulations where needed; then we can start new projects and initiatives. In this way, we can all move toward building a new Earth. You can read more about this and about how to contact us in our closing chapter, "Toward a New Earth."

OUR PERSONAL STORY

HOW DID WE START THIS?

My wife and I, together with many others, have been addressing issues we all have with money, survival, and work since 1989. I feel very passionate about creating a truly sustainable foundation for our financial and economic worlds. *I believe that money can become an abundant resource. Money exists to serve us, helping to direct our lives in a new way, being a portal for love, a great medium of exchange, and a solid support system for the well-being of all and of our beautiful planet Earth.*

The impact that money has on our life is huge. Understanding the way in which our monetary system and world economy works, as well as their shortcomings, is not easy. However, resolving our issues with money—and understanding how we can let it serve us and be used for the well-being of all life—is a key to the mystery of money. *It can turn the tide for our whole culture.*

And clearly, we ourselves need to take more responsibility for this. Abdicating responsibility to those who are selfish and greedy is what created the recent world financial crisis that almost resulted in a total meltdown of our monetary systems. This was a wake-up call we needed to hear, which forced us to take action. This book and the online platform we will build to accompany it are tools for us all to better understand what has gone wrong, and to give us a voice in how to work together to bring about positive change.

As soon as we feel that money is controlling our lives, it indicates that we have lost our lives somewhere. It is so important to understand that when we consider ourselves as victims of our monetary system or of those we consider to be in power, be they governments or big corporations, we need to remind ourselves of our *own* power. We need to realize that no one can tell us how to deal with money or behave with it. It is our communal creation and we as humanity need to resolve its mystery. *The world's money systems form a global commons, just as the ecosystems of the world are collectively owned and need our collective attention.*

THE START OF THE JOURNEY

My wife and I have been running a healing practice since 1983 and were a part of the emerging alternative, spiritual, new-age movement. In our movement, I had seen many positive experiences as a result of people being in a better world and leading a more harmonious life together. However, when it came to money, a lot of problems arose, and they were not so easy to resolve. I felt called through these different experiences to come face to face with money, to try to understand how it worked in our lives and how we could transform our issues around money. I felt compelled to create a workable, practical monetary road for us all, a road which creates true happiness, instead of creating the pain and conflict that I had witnessed.

My journey began with the feeling that I had no understanding of economics and money. Money seemed so elusive to me. I am sure many of you can relate to this. What I did feel was that I needed to start by looking at my fears in relation to money and at the fears of humanity as a whole. I felt that somehow I needed to overcome that fear and learn to replace it with love. This became a very profound process, involving all of my life's experiences. With deep inner transformational work, I managed to establish a foundation of love within. This meant that now I could look at all my questions around money from a much more stable perspective, from the experience of my heart and not from my fear.

Following this, in 1990 my wife and I decided to modify the financial exchanges we made in our healing practice. We had been asking for a fixed rate. Then we shifted, allowing people to support and care for us financially by making donations (considering their own situations and ours), thus making it possible for all to receive the help they needed, whatever their financial circumstances. We had no substantial savings, so it was quite an adventure! We could never calculate our income in advance and had to trust that somehow it would all work out—and it did. We were genuine in our attempt, people were very supportive of what we were doing, and this made our novel approach work. We loved, shared, and cared, and so did the others with us. The important part of doing this is that we had not just been moving from fear to love, *we had been moving from fear to trust.*

A LIFE-TRANSFORMING VISION

In 1994, I had an experience in the middle of the night: I saw money like an energy or atmosphere, as we sometimes see things in dreams. The whole atmosphere filled itself up with love. *Money and love became the same thing.* This opened up a whole new vista of possibilities for me, and we have explored this relationship ever since. My friend Barbara Wilder wrote her book *Money Is Love* inspired by this experience; she describes money as the bloodstream of the Earth. We can transform the flow of money into a flow of love.[6]

TWO STORIES ABOUT LEARNING TO TRUST

There are two stories I would like to share with you about what happened to us in 1997 when we moved to Scotland and started a small healing center and our charity, called World Finance Initiative. Until that time, my wife, Sandra, and I had always managed our financial lives very well and could always pay for everything and go wherever we needed to go. We had been successfully running our healing practice by donation up until then.

In early 1997, soon after we set up our charity, which was also founded on exploring the relationship between money and love, we took on a second home close to our healing practice. We found ourselves in the situation of not being able to pay the rent, which upset us. We couldn't reach our landlady to let her know. Two weeks later, still in the same financial situation, we felt inspired, together with an American friend who visited our center, Candice Powers, to manifest £2000 (about $3000) in three days!

Sandra and I both have been trained professionally in connecting to the spiritual worlds. Most of our lives we have been aware of being inwardly guided. Many people call it "listening to a still, small voice inside." At the end of three days, four gifts had come from supporters and friends whom we had spoken to by phone, and three gifts had come in the post from people who did not know anything about our situation. The total of these 7 gifts added up to £2000 to the penny!

It was an extraordinary experience for us. But that was not the end of the story. When we called our landlady and she heard about our problems with the rent, she said:

> If you sometimes can't pay it for one month, don't worry. I just read your newsletter. Bless you for doing such wonderful work! Unfortunately I will need to ask you for the rent, as I still have a loan with the bank, but I will let you know when the loan is paid off. You know the way I really feel about this whole situation is that I am so happy with the two of you in my home that I would rather pay you for staying there than ask you to pay me!

The second story is about something that happened half a year later. For the third time in the span of half a year, we found ourselves in financial difficulties. Behind our healing center there was a plot of woodland that needed a lot of care; it belonged to the local landowner. I had previously received permission from him to clear that woodland and use the wood for our fireplace. In the midst of this third small financial crisis, I heard very clear guidance advising me to go and clear the woodland, care for it, and trust the outcome. This happened three days in a row. I was nervous, because I needed money and could not see how it would come to us by clearing the woodland. But, at least I was giving time to the Earth, which does not always happen in our chase for money.

As I was working in the woodland, very powerful inspirations started, showing me the fundamentals of care-first. We were being taught about the relationship between money and care, which lies at the core of the all the work we have done since. As soon as the three days were over, a check unexpectedly arrived from a client of mine who I had helped previously, and who had not been able to make a contribution at the time I helped him. With that money, I traveled south to do my healing work, which created all the money we needed. The money arrived on time to solve our financial problem and all was sorted out.

In that first half year of creating our company, we had been in financial trouble three times. Since the third time, with the creation of Care First, we have never had the same financial difficulty again. What we learned was that the connection between money and love is not enough to create a new foundation for our economies. We also needed the connection between money and care to truly stabilize everything; *care is love in action.*

MOVING TOWARD WRITING THE BOOK

During the years that followed, we built up our vision called "The Garden, a Love-Based Economy, and a Care-First World." It inspired a lot of people, but the application of it was not so easy for many of them. In 2003, we developed a very powerful intensive workshop called "Meeting the Mystery of Money," which helped people to deal with their money issues on a very deep level. The workshop had a profound transformational effect and assisted people in applying the principles we teach. We have been very active with this in the United States, in the United Kingdom, and in the Netherlands. I also studied and began to actively work with bookkeeping and accountancy in business as a way to better understand our day-to-day use of money, business, and economics.

A few years ago, I felt that we needed to start to work on a much larger scale. I wanted to write a book, and this is where our adventure began. In March 2010, I met my friend and colleague Jon Freeman, author, consultant in organizational development, and director of the UK Centre for Human Emergence. Jon attended our workshop and felt our vision needed to be shared worldwide. He says in the acknowledgments of his 2010 book, *Future Money: The Way We Survive Global Bankruptcy:*

> It is Louis Böhtlingk who triggered this book, which was not part of my plans. Although I had been developing a close interest in economics from the time of the credit crunch onward, it was Louis' vision of a "care-first" world, and his beautiful, elegant articulation of the transition that we are making, which pushed my button. He has the mythos of the

change, to which this book [*Future Money*] supplies something of the logos, and the content began to formulate itself during conversations with him. His vision is very much "an idea whose time has come" and the first impulse behind this book was to support him. He and his partner Sandra are above all people who practice what they preach.[7]

PART ONE

THE GARDEN

CHAPTER 1

MY INTENTION AND MY JOURNEY

MY INTENTION

I am writing this book
with the intention for all humanity
to see and dream a vision
of a new economic foundation
and be able to implement it.

I believe that our need for vision is deep
and I want to make my contribution toward it
by sharing insights and revelations I received over the years
in my search for an answer to the question:
How we can resolve our financial and economic issues and
establish peace on Earth?

I was born near Leiden, in the Netherlands, in 1950. My father was the youngest PhD in the Netherlands at the time. I lost him when I was eight and a half in a car accident. My mother could not cope with my father's death and was taken in for treatment several times, as I grew up. She was a very loving, caring, and selfless human being. Considering her beautiful nature, it was hard for me as a child to understand why she needed to have so much pain. Later in life, I understood that we learn through pain and that in that sense pain can be seen as a door, an opportunity for growth. My wife Sandra and I apply this concept all the time in our soul reading and healing practice, which we have been running since 1984. There is always hope and light available to help us master the difficult and painful things we meet in life.

Since 1989, I have been looking at the issues we all have with money, survival, and work, to which I have applied that same principle that I applied in my healing practice. In today's difficult economic and financial circumstances, I know there is a door, a way through for us all, and a way in which we can resolve this situation together.

In October 2010, I came in contact with Hazel Henderson—author, world-renowned futurist, and evolutionary economist. She is a wonderful and powerful lady from St. Augustine in Florida, who has been working with these issues for a lifetime.[8] We decided to work together. She offered to assist me with the writing of this book; for this purpose, I decided to visit her for 21 days in November 2010. My narrative and voyage of discovery for this book started with my journey to the United States.

MY JOURNEY

Friday Nov 5th, 2010: As I am leaving the Groningen train station on my way to the airport, I am struck by a big poster on the platform of one of stations I pass. Below this fascinating image, it says:

Follow your heart
Use your head
Triodos Bank

Figure 1.1 A Triodos Bank poster. The translated message says, "Follow your heart/Use Your Head/Triodos Bank."

Triodos Bank is a Dutch bank. It was voted the most sustainable bank on this planet in 2009. Triodos started as a savings bank, but now offers a full range of banking, investment, and customer accounts. The bank has been in business since 1980 and operates in Holland, Belgium, Great Britain, Spain, and Germany (see Chapter 13).

My flight to the United States was a few days after the midterm elections in the United States. This was a time when the US economy was in bad shape; many people were losing their jobs and their homes. On the plane I thought: "This book is not mine. It is ours. It is our common ground. *Together we can rebuild our world economy and financial system.*"

As I was taken by shuttle to my hotel, the driver and I got to talking about the present state of the economy in the United States, and I explained to him about care-first. "In care-first," I said, "money is being used in service of the well-being of people and the Earth, and not at their expense. Care leads the way and money operates in service of that care. In business, care-first is all about care for our employees, customers, and suppliers, for the product or service we provide and for the environment.

Care is in the driver's seat. Businesses who operate like this are often very successful."

We spoke during the ride about whether governments or large companies would think this way, about socially responsible investing (SRI) and the mortgage system in the United States. I told him about the Triodos poster I had seen at the Dutch train station. He had never heard of such a bank. We were both aware of the fact that the mainstream media do not cover much of this good news in the world.

The more we talked, the more we felt that, when care-first becomes the modus operandi in economics, we will be able to resolve many issues. We also realized that many of us, because of the need to survive, are very accustomed to just thinking about ourselves and our own needs and benefits. The basic care for ourselves and our relations is care-first, but when we pursue the need for money at the expense of the well-being of ourselves and others and do not love our work, we really enter the realm of money-first.

I told him about our workshop "Meeting the Mystery of Money," where we deal with all these issues, and where almost everyone attending agrees with our vision for a care-first world, but always wonder how we can make it happen in the "real" world. I said: "It is a positive sign though, that at least we all agree on what we would like to see happening. It is my hope that my book will assist the process of *redesigning the world, as we know it*. A lawyer friend of mine from Washington, DC, said something to me in 1998, which I never forgot: "Eighty percent of the people want to care and would support your idea; 60 percent of that 80 percent only know how to operate within the current system; 20 percent of that 80 percent might have woken up to the idea that we can do things differently. The really greedy people on this planet are a small minority."

When we arrived at the hotel, the taxi driver and I agreed to stay in touch. On Saturday, Nov 5th, 2010, I met Hazel for the first time and the writing of the book began. Hazel has been speaking about a love economy since 1982. We decided to create *Dare to Care* as a roadmap to a positive future for economics and finance. The book is based on my vision piece "The Garden, a Love-Based Economy, and a Care-First World," which is the starting point for the three parts of the book and contains most of the poetry you will read here.

Part 1: The Garden. We all love our gardens. Some gardens look like a dream. Many gardens give us a sense of peace. The Garden I speak of relates to an economy we dream of, where our highest ideals are fulfilled.

The Garden is the space in which we all work together to make this transformation happen and to build our new world. It is the world of our hearts. It is where we receive our dreams, where we visualize our world, where we think about it and wonder how to create it. It is the birthing ground, where we motivate ourselves to build, where we actively work together and make our decisions. It is also the world of the Earth, of Nature, of our home, the world we come from and return to. You can also call it the world of spirit, of heaven, of heaven on Earth. The Garden is a cocoon in which we create our world; it is a laboratory of life.

Part 2: The Love-Based Economy. The love-based economy is the grounding of those ideals. We will look at this in detail. It is a new foundation for economics that we can all understand.

The love-based economy is an intellectual and emotional inner structure or temple we create. This is the foundation for all our work, for all the exchanges we make (both monetary and nonmonetary). It is what underpins all economic activity. It is the foundation underlying all trading, all business, all financial institutions and governments. It is the mirror in which we can see reflected whether we are moving in the right direction and are creating a sustainable future or not. This love translates itself into principles we can all apply and live by, through which we can make what we dream in our Garden real. Such an economy is the foundation for our whole culture.

Part 3: A Care-First World. A care-first world is one in which caring leads the way and money serves the care; where we become conscious of our money-first actions (using money at the expense of care) and learn to transform them.

The care-first world is the road to freedom for our financial world. *Care-first is the measure by which we can see where our use of money is destructive or constructive, whether we are serving the well-being of people and the Earth or not.* It is the place where we are being tested in relation to how we use money and create money, how we create our mechanisms of exchange, whether we do it with current or complementary currencies or use nonmonetary exchanges. It is the world of application, where we practice

7

what we preach, the portal to our new world, to the future and the Garden. Through care-first we can return home and create the world we want and dream of. Here we create our love-based economy and can enter into the Garden by right action.

CHAPTER 2

OWNERSHIP AND THE GIFTS OF THE EARTH

It is vitally important to dream and to visualize what we want, even if things are not looking good. In 1987, I had an experience, reflected in my verses below, that became the foundation for most of my thinking around economics. *It was the experience of seeing everything the Earth provides as a gift to us all.* Many of us feel that we all have an equal right to shelter, food, education, and health care, which is a feeling of justice, fairness, and care. This is connected to the experience I had of the living presence of the Earth, loving us equally and unconditionally and wanting us all to enjoy its gifts.

Ownership has become a completely natural thing to us.
We own our car, our home, and our material possessions.
But what is ownership in light of all that the Earth materially provides?
Do we own the planet? Do we own life? Do we own our children?
Can we own a gift?

I had an inner experience on Christmas 1987.
I was thinking about how we are using up the resources of this planet so quickly,
when suddenly I felt a surge of love rising up from below,
which I experienced as the love of Mother Earth,
the Mother aspect of creation.

I felt that all material things are the expression of this love
and that we can learn to receive her love for us all.
I felt that once I truly received it, all I could do is share it.
Then I experienced that ownership, that saying to her gift "this is mine,"
was almost like an insult to the love being offered.

In Native American culture, they know that we do not own this planet.
Chief Seattle said, in his speech, when the white man proposed to buy their land,[9]
"How can you buy and sell the sky, the warmth of the land. The idea is strange to us.
If we do not own the freshness of the air and the sparkle of the water,
how can we buy them?"

"Every part of the Earth is sacred to my people.
Every shining pine needle, every sandy shore,
every mist in the dark wood, every clearing
and humming insect is holy
in the memory and experience of my people."

"So, if we sell our land, love it as we have loved it.
Care for it as we have cared for it.
Hold in your mind the memory of the land as it is when you take it.
And with all your strength, with all your mind, with all your heart,
preserve it for your children and love it, as God loves us."

When we say, "this is mine" in a possessive way
we separate ourselves from the Source, ourselves and the rest of the world.
When we are not grateful
and want to show off with all our material goods
we are alone and without love.

As soon as we receive the gift in gratitude,
we feel connected to the Source, to ourselves and
our world and are full of love.
Possessiveness creates separation,
but when we steward (take care of) the Earth we are one with all life.

It is nice to have our own home and privacy,
but it remains still a part of the Whole
and of all life and is never really our possession.
It remains the gift it is.
A gift for all, one part of which we can care for.

It is so natural for us to want to share. In our workshop "Meeting the Mystery of Money," many people express how upset they feel about inequality on this planet, with so many people living in poverty while others have way too much. Sharing is not a foundational aspect of our present economic situation; I feel that this is one of the main reasons why such profound inequality exists and why the gap between the rich and the poor has been with us for such a long time.

All our work, wherever we do it is based on the implementation of Four Actions, four movements or shifts that we can make to move from one level of experience and consciousness to another. They assist us to move toward an economy that is truly sustainable, fair, and caring. We have worked with these actions since 1996 and they remain consistent in their essence.

First action: *To move from a place where we feel driven to acquire*
and take our part of the gift,
to embracing that gift together and receiving and sharing it.
Second action: *To move from ownership to stewardship.*
Third action: *To move from the use of money based on*
our greed, fear, desire for power, selfishness, and possessiveness
to the use of money based
on caring, sharing, loving, giving, and receiving.
Fourth action: *To move from a money-first attitude to a care-first attitude.*

The first two actions are about living on a beautiful planet
and how we can share its gifts and take care of them together.
The third and fourth actions are connected to
the transformation of finance and using money in a different way.

11

THE GIFTS OF LIFE ON EARTH AND THE GIFT WE ARE

I experience these gifts as a foundation for our lives
but I also feel gratitude for what we have been given.
We are being loved and we are love itself.
The devastation we cause with war, hunger, and pollution
is very disturbing and ultimately is not consistent with the gifts we receive.

The pain we can create by the way that we deal with money is a part of this.
War, hunger, and pollution show our current destructive behavior.
We can also apply money in a constructive manner.
By shifting the way we perceive and use money, we can begin
to restore ourselves and our planet to a more basic harmony.

That is how money can help
to create peace instead of war,
to create plenty for all and to stop hunger,
to restore the ecosystem of the Earth
instead of endangering it.

Money can be moved by the power of the heart
by love and care,
by sharing and giving and receiving
and it can take us back into the Garden,
take us back home.

The gifts we receive, the gifts we share,
the gifts we steward;
the consciousness of these gifts, the awareness of these gifts,
the experience of these gifts
can all lead us home.

The experience of these gifts and our gratitude for them
can infuse all our economic and financial thinking
and can restore the harmony we lost.
Living with and respecting these gifts can rebalance
all that has gone out of balance.

Acknowledging the gift is a very important component
of what makes a true economy function.
The unconditional nature of any gift is very important,
and this is what my experience was with Mother Earth:
the unconditional nature of what she provides.

Can we provide that for each other?
Can we create a foundation that sustains us all, just like Mother Earth does?
Shall we let our hearts speak
and make it happen?
A gift lightens up the heart both when we receive it and when we give it.

I want to share some more quotes from Freeman's book *Future Money*:

> Cultures which have remained closer to the natural world continue to recognise themselves as caretakers of the garden. It would seem that when we gave our power to the God of Money, we left the garden. It is time for us to go back. Our way back is by replacing a money-first world with a care-first world. All the items on our list of requirements for future money will be fulfilled when both our thinking and our systems embody that care, when we apply the principle of stewardship to balance the needs of all life. Those requirements arise out of a choice to care for each other, for ourselves, for the planet's other life-forms, for its resources, for its climate and its oceans.[10] ...And we will need money. We will need a fair, flexible and responsive system with which to express our real Values and support our sharing of the Earth's Gifts.[11]
>
> ...The historical picture is one in which we have allowed money to become master. We have made it into a god, and developed belief systems in which we put the money first.[12] ...The money-first world is coming to an end because it has neither made us happy, nor established a means by which billions of humans can live sustainably.[13]

. . . The conscious choice is our first step, our deliberate decision to put the money-first world behind us. What follows has to be a re-engagement with the feminine, the heart-centred knowing that engages our deep humanity. That instinctive response is also the one which feeds the human spirit reawakens our love for ourselves, for each other and for the Earth.[14]

CHAPTER 3

HAZEL'S CAKE AND MEASURING GROSS DOMESTIC PRODUCT

Hazel Henderson created the picture of a cake with four layers to give us a depiction of our economy, shown in Figure 3.1. In a video made about Hazel's life, Nathalie Beekman, the producer, says: "She invented the concept of a Love Economy and compared [the visualization of] her theory to a four-dimensional cake."[15]

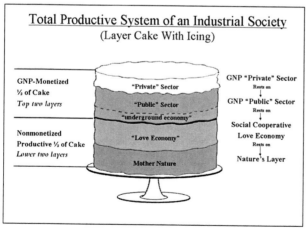

Figure 3.1 Total productive system of an industrial society (layer cake with icing). Copyright 1982 Hazel Henderson. All rights reserved.

In the video, Hazel says:

> The first layer is the private sector, which is the icing on the cake. We all like to be free to innovate. Supporting this layer is the Public sector, the taxpayers' supported infrastructure, which businesses have to have, whether it is [for] ports, airports, hospitals, schools, and roads. These first two layers are really the only thing economists calculate in money terms and what makes up the Gross National Product and Gross Domestic Product.
>
> But, of course, there are two hidden layers underneath that support the whole structure, but they are completely off the books and that is what I call the Love Economy, which is all the unpaid work that women do to raise children, all the household work, serving on the school board, and all the voluntary work. In industrial societies this is at least fifty percent of all the production that goes on and in developing countries it is sometimes as much as seventy percent (UN, Human Development Index 1995). Then the entire structure is supported by Nature's productivity, which is the bottom layer.

A friend of Hazel's, Riane Eisler, wrote a wonderful book, The Real Wealth of Nations.[16] She describes this real wealth as the people and the Earth. She also uses a similar picture to Hazel's, which she describes as the old and new economic map (see Figure 3.2).

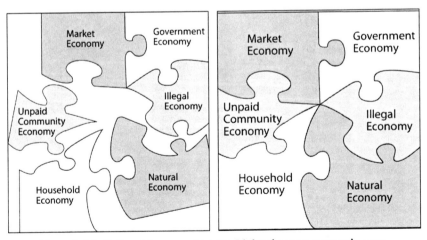

Figure 3.2 Left: the old economic map. Right: the new economic map.

Riane Eisler says: "In the old economic models, the foundational economic sectors—household [economy], unpaid community [economy] and natural [economy]—are omitted, which leads to distorted views and policies. Our challenge is to develop a caring economics where human needs and capacities are nurtured, our natural habitat is conserved, and our great capacity for caring and creativity is supported."[17]

What I realized, when I absorbed these pictures, is that we're almost totally conditioned to look at economics only in terms of money. We overlook what the Earth does and, in many ways, what women do, which is often unpaid work. Everything we do in the financial and economic worlds is supported by what the Earth and what the women at home provide. Without these two aspects of our economy there would not be any cake to enjoy!

Over the years, I realized that so many of the answers I received to the problems we have with money and our economies were based on what are traditionally considered feminine qualities: caring, sharing, loving, giving, and receiving. As a man, this was sometimes difficult for me. I just wanted to get on with things, but felt deeply that these qualities had to lead the way for us, to resolve our issues. I recently heard a beautiful expression: "We are in the era of the young maiden," indicating the rising of the feminine energies in our manifested world.

I want to focus a great deal of attention on the financial world, which as Hazel describes in her cake diagram, mainly exists in the top two layers of her "cake"—the private and the public sector. Many of the problems we face with finance and economics are created by the structure and mechanics of the financial world. What does our financial world really look like? How do we create money and use it? How do we build and destroy with it? What kind of system would we like to have?

The Four Actions that we promote are grounded in the two bottom layers of Hazel's cake. They are all related to the Earth and to our caring values. These actions can help to transform the two top layers, which make up our financial world. I pay a lot of attention to the quality of each financial transaction we make and how it affects the Earth and all of us as a community.

I will give you an example. We work together in a small group of people (community), are happy with how we make our financial exchanges, and can all see clearly what we do together. Suddenly, someone gets a smart idea by which he or she can make more money, but does this by taking from what flows between us and using it to his or her own advantage, either by charging too much interest or by making too much profit (whatever the trick consists of). We will all see this immediately, and it shows up as bad behavior within the harmonious life we have led together. We can then correct it. We had an example of this in the Netherlands, where a top CEO of a main bank, which had received 22 billion euros of bailout money from the government, drew a one-million euro bonus on top of a one-million euro salary. This infuriated the customers of the bank so much that the CEO withdrew the bonus.

I have often said that what is missing in our world is that *we do not seem to have a shared moral code about what we can and cannot do with money.* We can get away with very greedy behavior and actions and sometimes are even admired for it. We look at how much money someone made, without asking ourselves how the money was made, and at what cost. We seem to have lost or forsaken the lessons we all learned as small children.

This is the same with the effect of our transactions on the Earth. How did the financial transactions we just made affect the Earth? Are we taking more than we return from the Earth and our communities? Do we create any damage? What is the effect of each financial transaction we make on the whole? (See more about this in Chapter 10, Twelve Questions to Ask About a Financial Transaction.)

To complete this chapter, I would like to pay some attention to the work that both Riane Eisler and Hazel Henderson do to measure the Gross Domestic Product (GDP)[18] and Gross National Product (GNP)[19] in a clearer, more honest manner than they usually are viewed. I quote Judith D. Schwartz from her article "Is GDP an Obsolete Measure of Progress?" which appeared in *Time* magazine, January 30, 2010:[20]

> Since last summer [2009] the nation's Gross Domestic Product (GDP) has gone up—indeed, it grew at a surprising 5.7% rate in the 4th quarter—seeming to confirm what we've been hearing: the recession is officially over. But wait—foreclosure and unemployment rates remain high

and food banks are seeing record demand. Could it be that the GDP, that gold standard of economic data, might not be the best way to gauge a nation's relative prosperity? Since it became the prime economic indicator during the Second World War (to monitor war production) many have criticized policy-makers' reliance on the GDP—and proposed substitute measures. For example, there is the Human Development Index (HDI), used by the UN's Development Programme, which considers life expectancy and literacy as well as standard of living as determined by GDP. And the Genuine Progress Indicator, which incorporates aspects of social welfare such as income equity, pollution, and access to health care. In the international community, perhaps the biggest nudge has come from French President Nicolas Sarkozy, who commissioned a report by marquee-name economists, including Nobel Laureates Joseph Stiglitz and Amartya Sen, to find alternatives to what he calls "GDP fetishism."[21]

What exactly have we been fetishizing? Basically, market activity and growth. The GDP generally expressed as a per-capita figure and often adjusted to reflect purchasing power, represents the market value of goods and services produced within a nation's boundaries. That sounds reasonable, until we consider what it doesn't measure: the general progress in health and education, the condition of public infrastructure, fuel efficiency, community and leisure.[22]

"It's a narrow calculation of cash flow," says Hazel Henderson, President of Ethical Markets Media (USA and Brazil) and who co-developed the Calvert-Henderson Quality of Life Indicators, which unbundles, rather than averages, 12 indicators. "Because it's averaged, the GDP mystifies and masks the gap between rich and poor. I don't think there's ever been such a large disconnect between the GDP and what ordinary people are experiencing."

THE QUALITY OF LIFE INDICATORS

A more accurate quality of life assessment is the Calvert–Henderson Quality of Life Indicators. A quote from their website (*www.calvert-henderson.com*) notes that:

> Our Indicators range far beyond the traditional national accounts of GNP and GDP and other money-denominated indexes on inflation (CPI) [Consumer Price Indicator], incomes, interest rates, trade deficits, and the national budget.[23] In the same way we've developed and use the Gross National Product to measure the growth of the economy, we should develop and use a scorecard of new indicators for holding politicians responsible for progress toward other national goals, like improving education, extending health care, preserving the environment, and making the military meet today's needs.

About this indicator, Prof. Mihaly Csikszentmihalyi observed (also on their website): "The Calvert-Henderson Quality of Life Indicators is one of the most hopeful developments of recent times. We desperately need tools to assess the true human well-being with more than monetary, material measures."

Riane Eisler's wonderful website for the Center for Partnership Studies (CPS), *www.partnershipway.org*, challenges us to join the 30-million member Coalition backing the CPS-commissioned Urban Institute Recommendations on Caring Economics. The GDP keeps rising, but joblessness doesn't drop and child care and educational budgets are slashed. On behalf of the millions of people they represent across the United States, CPS calls for immediate action for supplementing the GDP with new measurements—and solutions—based on the findings and recommendations of the report, "The State of Society: Measuring Economic Success and Human Well-Being,"[24] commissioned by the CPS and released in June 2010.

CHAPTER 4

ALONE AND TOGETHER IN OUR SURVIVAL ISSUES

O n my third morning in Florida, I found myself speaking with two other guests. They pointed out that St. Augustine is the oldest town in the United States, founded in 1565. It is the place where the first settlers landed. We were talking about the book I was writing and I thought: *Can we rebuild our economy and financial world and enter a new land together and become new inhabitants of a world we all love to live in?*

One of the hotel guests was a psychotherapist. After listening to my description of the book, he said: "This whole thing around money is about survival and when we Americans survive, we will do anything to do so: we will defend and attack. It brings out a primal force in us. When you want to connect us to care and [to] warmer ideas, you need to know this. When we need to make a living, we can be tough."

I said to him: "In our workshop 'Meeting the Mystery of Money" we address that core survival level and allow everyone to look at their fears, desperation, anger, loneliness, and conditioning. We look at what makes us tick when it comes to money. In the past, the man needed to hunt to provide for his family or grow food; now he needs to get money. That is his bottom line. When we deal with hungry children in the Third World it is the same: They just need to be fed. Then they can start to think and work towards their dreams and ideals."

One of the questions we ask people in our big workshop is: "Look at your fears in relationship to your life with money. What is your deepest fear?" Just take a moment, if you wish, and ask yourself that question.

The responses we hear the most are: "That I will be on my own without anything," "That I will end up broke and out on the street," "That I will have not have enough income as I become elderly."

As the workshop progresses, something else comes forward, which is that *many people feel deeply unsupported and alone in the survival game;* they feel that they need to do it all on their own. For many of us, money is a very private matter and therefore we do not always share our situation with others. Someone said to me many years ago: "It is more difficult for people to talk about their money situation than it is to talk about sex."

It is clear to me that there is much more we can do to support one another. I sometimes jokingly say: "Shall I do your surviving? Then you can do mine!" The loneliness and struggle we can experience in needing to make money for ourselves and for our loved ones is not easy to bear. In order to survive, almost all of us need jobs. Jobs provide us and our families with the money we need. You often hear: "I'll take any job in hard times to support myself and my family. I hope enough jobs are being created for us all, so that we can make ends meet."

Jobs can be the activities we love to do. They can be the expression of the unique contribution each of us can and wants to make; the expression of what we are passionate about. When we are working just to survive and make money, but do not love what we do, *we are creating a world that is not ours.* Then the money rules us and this creates unhappiness and frustration.

When we talk about these wonderful ideas of sharing and caring and doing the work we love, but we do not resolve that survival pressure that we experience, it is hard to live with these beautiful ideas. *Therefore I feel that it is important to make our number-one priority the four basic survival needs we all have: the need for a home, for food, for education, and for health care.* We need to ensure that these four basic needs and human rights are being fulfilled for all; that we can organize our financial and economic world in such a way that we know we are all being taken care of; it is so important that we all take care of each other. Eleanor Roosevelt initiated these basic human rights in *The Universal Declaration of Human Rights.*

This foundation of basic care for each other reflects what I call Mother Earth's love for us all; it can become our focus. Although it is very important to talk about how we fulfill these four basic needs for everyone, I feel we should never lose sight of the goal itself.

One core principle I believe is that people don't deserve to do work they do not love just to make money. We need to help each other to bring out our best, using our real talents in our work, and let our work support us financially. People should not receive a college education only to do work they hate because they need money. Nor should people perform in unskilled work that they do not really want to do, without the possibility of further education. When that basic survival need is satisfied, we can relax. We have our home, food, and our children taken care of. We can educate ourselves and take care of our health. Only then have we created a solid foundation for life. Then a big part of what we need spiritually and materially falls into place and we can live and work from this new foundation. As a world community, we can then create this for everyone and make sure that our brothers and sisters in other countries have the same opportunity. *We can do this by working for and creating the money needed to provide for ourselves, and by being supported financially through the sharing of resources.*

I am sure this can be made to work financially. The amounts of money that are generated through practices where we are just making more money out of money, like currency trading and stock market transactions, are phenomenal. In 2009 the derivatives market alone (see Chapter 12) had an estimated value of $630 trillion (according to Jon Freeman).[25] We just need to decide what we want to do and how to channel money in the right way. It is finding that balance between how we take care of ourselves and each other and how we create our own income, while supporting each other financially. It is the balance between basic income (see Chapter 6) and starting our own business, as in the microcredit movement (see Chapter 13). *Basic income* is an income unconditionally granted to all, providing everyone with a foundation for right livelihood.[26] In the microcredit movement, people are coming out of poverty by creating their own businesses to provide for their basic livelihood themselves.

I would love us to think about these questions together and find optimal solutions. How can we stabilize our financial and economic world so that, instead of creating something that does not serve us and goes against our basic nature and at times drives us crazy, it creates happiness and a deep sense of satisfaction? How are we going to feel supported and know that we can lean on one another? There is no reason for us to remain in the hell we are creating together.

We can reach out to one another from the isolation we are in, share our gifts, and let the money circulate. I watched Desmond Tutu in a YouTube video from 2006, when he addressed members of the Basic Income Earth Network. It was a very moving delivery, in which he shared how we can reach out to one another and not leave each other hanging over the abyss, and how we all can be treated with dignity. Here are some excerpts from his talk:

> This is a topic that is very close to my heart. You see, we stand at a historic crossroads: one road leads up to the higher ground of social equity and inclusion, human dignity, full economic participation, broad based prosperity and growth. The other leads downwards to growing poverty and economic inequity, social conflict, increased joblessness, and pervasive insecurity. The high road involves time-honored values of solidarity, compassion, and care. The low road is characterized by selfishness and greed. It threatens the stability of our families and even our entire social fabric. We have a unique opportunity to wipe out hunger and abject poverty; to make sure that no one falls into absolute destitution. For perhaps the first time in history we have the resources and know-how to make starvation and dependency relics of the past. But do we have the will? We can achieve this vision, if only we can learn to use the wealth and resources entrusted to us to build real human security . . .
>
> A lasting stable security comes from a healthy and educated people [who are] able to look up at themselves and their families together with the assurance that, should they fall, there is a net of compassion and care to catch them and a springboard to lift them to more sustaining livelihoods . . .

Friends, I do not need to remind you of the importance and benefits of campaigns, such as the basic income movement, that are designed to enhance the dignity, well-being, and inclusion of all people and to move us closer to our vision of social equity. Let me rather thank you for your shared commitment to this noble goal."[27]

We are living together on this planet with all that is available to us. In that togetherness, we can learn how to share the gifts bestowed upon us: all that the Earth provides and the talents we have been given.

We can affirm among ourselves that we all have an equal right to housing, food, education, and health care and make sure *that everyone has enough in every country*; that whatever economic and financial structures we live in, we commit to making this our focus and our bottom line. This will help to stabilize the world economy and create the opportunity for all of us to share our gifts. The challenge is to agree to make that choice, and then work out how to implement it. *In the process of doing so, we are tackling the whole financial world we've created.*

We need to create an understanding of how we can live in harmony with money and let our financial resources serve us in achieving our highest objectives. Eleanor Roosevelt initiated the entry of these four basic needs into *The Universal Declaration of Human Rights*, passed December 10, 1948, at the United Nations General Assembly. Below are parts of Articles 25, 26 and Article 1:

Article 25. (1) Everyone has the right to a standard of living adequate for the health and well-being of himself and of his family, including food, clothing, housing and medical care and necessary social services, and the right to security in the event of unemployment, sickness, disability, widowhood, old age, or other lack of livelihood in circumstances beyond his control.

Article 26. (1) Everyone has the right to education. Education shall be free, at least in the elementary and fundamental stages. Elementary education shall be compulsory. Technical and professional education shall be made generally available and higher education shall be equally accessible to all on the basis of merit.

Article 1. All human beings are born free and equal in dignity and rights. They are endowed with reason and conscience and should act towards one another in a spirit of brotherhood. [28]

CHAPTER 5

MEETING THE MYSTERY OF MONEY

In our workshop "Meeting the Mystery of Money," people find out that they are not alone, that we share very similar issues, because we hear each other's stories. Our workshop provides everyone with a space to really investigate their relationship to money and look at their money, work, and survival issues. There is a space for all of us to share our deepest fears, concerns, pains, and issues, and from there we can move forward into the future together.

We portray the tests we all go through with money by using archetypal figures, imaginary characters, to which we give roles, each representing different aspects of ourselves in relation to that test. It is very serious, but also a lot of fun. We all can move so easily into our heads when we think and talk about money. The workshop provides a space to be with our hearts, emotions, body, soul, and spirit and a chance to look at our lives with money in a new way.

The archetypes are a God of Money; a Prince of Peace; a Goddess of Abundance, representing Mother Earth; a Community Keeper; a Condor; and an Eagle. There is a Native American prophecy which says that when the Condor and Eagle fly together, it is a sign of peace on Earth. The Condor represents the heart; the Eagle represents the head.

During the workshop, we all come face to face with the God of Money, who represents our fear, greed, selfishness, possessiveness, and desire for power. But he shows himself also as a compassionate god, who creates the space for us to have these experiences and learn. He also says about himself: "I asked you to do business. I asked you to build an empire. I helped to build the world, but my weakness was that I lived without love, that I lived without the Goddess (Mother Earth)."

Later in the workshop, the Goddess says, "The destructive aspect of our use of money is when we do anything without care. *We have always had the choice to care or not to care and many times we decided not to care.* Maybe it wasn't conscious in us; maybe we thought there was no choice and that we had to get money at whatever expense. But then we slowly learned that we can't use that as an excuse for harming ourselves, each other, and Mother Earth."

As we work on these parts of ourselves and our relationship to money, we become aware of the God of Money as the portal to a new life. As we clear our fear and greed and move forward towards the loving, caring, and sharing aspects of ourselves, the God of Money slowly dies in us and we enter a new land, which we can call the Garden. When everyone has come face to face with the God of Money in the workshop, *the God of Money dies and is reborn as the Prince of Peace,* who then marries the Goddess of Abundance, and they lead us into the new world together.

Just before the God of Money dies, he says, "My role is over. I have destroyed what I needed to destroy. I will withdraw. Everything I have built will fall apart. I am an illusion in the human mind. Instead of creating separation, I now invite you to unite, to bring everything together again, to create true community on this Earth." Here he shows himself as *a door to a higher level of community.* All of us join again after our very individualized path in his kingdom, but come together in community, based on the strength gained by our individuation.

The God of Money represents the part of us that looks for money without caring, the part that goes off on a tangent and says, "It is just me and my money, that is all that matters. I don't care about what happens to the rest or our planet." However, this behavior is also a learning ground; we can all go through this indifference one way or the other. We all go through our test with money-first (using money at the expense of caring) and care-first (using money in service of caring) all the time, every second of every day.

In the workshop there is never any judgment toward anyone's actions or behavior. We can all decide for ourselves what these actions are and what we want to do with them.

When we arrive in the new land together in our workshop-imagination-play, the God of Money, now reborn as the Prince of Peace, says to us all:

> What I have destroyed needs to be rebuilt. You can live your dreams on this planet and you can create a beautiful use of money. Money now expresses your heart. Money is not separate from it. You create all the money that flows through your life, and you can choose how you manifest it. You are in a free relationship to me. You can make me real in your life, you can change me, and you can do with me what you like. Don't feel you are dependent upon the present money system. A system is just people deciding how they create and use money. You are free to live differently. Money can take many forms.
>
> During our time together, I have been the threshold. Understand that I have a function. When you pass through me, you come to understand that you can choose to create your world. When you pass through me, you move from fear to love and from separation to unity. You become a family of caring, sharing, loving, giving, and receiving members. This family holds hands in a different way. This family is truly together. This family doesn't own the planet. This family lets money be there for everyone. This family shares the gift. I am now serving the process of creating a new flow of money. A flow of love. A flow that can heal wounds.

At some point, the Goddess of Abundance says, "We chase money and feel we have no choice. It is what we call the *real world*—a world outside of ourselves that makes us suffer. *And then we realize that we invented money, that we decided to use it at some point and that we have the power to redesign it, that we can change what we agreed.* We begin to see that destruction is not needed, that somehow we can approach money differently."

It is very clear that many of us feel victimized by the money system we are a part of, by the world we live in. So many will say in desperation, "But can we really do anything about it?"

That feeling is understandable. We can do everything about it, and that is my reason for writing this book. I know that together we can change our financial and economic world. It is not that we are just being controlled by a few in power. When we feel we are controlled by them, we allow that to happen. We have the power to allow that to continue, or we can choose to do something about it!

We all stand in front of this God of Money in the same way, with the same test, with the same capacity for conscience and heart. Let's support each other to go where we choose to go.

In our workshop, *the Condor and Eagle represent the portal to the new land*. As John Perkins, a US economist, activist, and author, said about the prophecy of the Condor and the Eagle:

> In the beginning of 1968 I started working in the Amazon. Since then I have lived and worked with indigenous cultures all over the planet. Every one of them has a prophecy that we have arrived at a time for the potential of tremendous transformation. The one I like the best, because I think it is the most succinct and eloquent, in a way, is that of the Condor and the Eagle. This comes out of the Amazon, way back thousands and thousands of years ago. Nobody has any idea when this prophecy started, but it worked its way up into the Andes to Central America, the Mayan and Aztec cultures, and up into Hopi culture, right up to Northern America across the Bering Strait; and you find reminiscence of it in the Asian Steppe.
>
> It basically says that back in the mist of history, human societies decided to go on two different paths. One was the path of the Condor, which is really the path of the heart, of the intuition, of the feminine path, if you want to [call it that], and the other one was the path of the Eagle, which is the path of the mind, of the science, of the industrial, perhaps you could even say of the masculine. They went their separate routes and then in one period of history it

was forecast, thousands of years ago, it was prophesized that in the eight pachacuti—a pachacuti is a 500-year period, which would begin in 1490s—the Eagle's people would become so powerful that they would practically drive the Condor people into extinction. And we know this happened. After Columbus, the industrial people, the people of science, practically drove the indigenous people into extinction. But the prophecy goes on to say that during the next pachacuti—the next 500-year period, starting at the beginning of the 1990s—we will arrive at a time with the potential for the two to come together, for the Eagle and the Condor to fly in one sky, to mate, to dance together and to create a whole new level of consciousness, and so we are in that time now.

The prophecies don't say that it will happen, they say that we are at the time of potential and it is up to us to make it happen.[29]

John Perkins is someone who has experienced our financial and economic practices in its worst expressions, as described in his bestselling book *Confessions of an Economic Hit Man*, which gives a very honest account of his own life experiences and is quite an eye-opener. His life is an example of the redemptive process that the God of Money in us goes through as he resurrects himself into the Prince of Peace.

We all can walk through our darkness, leave it behind, and walk forward into a brighter future. I have often said: *"When we, as humanity, pass our test with the God of Money, we enter the Garden."*

So, although we create a lot of harm with our behavior and definitely do not always change willingly, we all can come to terms with our human nature. We need to assist one another to come forward with our best and we also need to redeem our actions by rebuilding what we've destroyed in our own lives, in the lives of others, and on our planet. Let's enter a space of compassion together.

CHAPTER 6

COMMUNITY-BASED INITIATIVES

I would like to call your attention to some very successful and long-standing community-based initiatives all around the globe, which address how we can live together and how we can run our economic and financial lives. I view some of these projects as living laboratories, in which new mechanisms and ways of living are being developed for our future.

GLOBAL ECOVILLAGE NETWORK (GEN)

Many of these initiatives are brought together under the umbrella of an organization called the Global Ecovillage Network (GEN). They say on their website (*www.gen.ecovillage.org*):

> The Global Ecovillage Network offers inspiring examples of how people and communities can live healthy, coopera-tive, genuinely happy and meaningful lifestyles —beacons of hope that help in the transition to a more sustainable future on Earth. We foster a culture of mutual respect, shar-ing, inclusiveness, positive intent, and fair energy exchange.

The GEN is a global confederation of people and communities that meet and share their ideas, exchange technologies, develop cultural and educational exchanges, publish directories and newsletters, and are dedicated to restoring the land and living "sustainable plus" lives by putting more back into the environment than they take out. Founded in 1996, GEN is a grassroots nonprofit organization that links together a highly diverse worldwide movement of autonomous ecovillages and related projects.

What are ecovillages? Ecovillages are communities of people who strive to live sustainably, integrating supportive social relations with ecological design practices. They seek to explore a way of life that fosters harmony between people and with nature, renewing the living systems of the planet, and nurturing the full development of each person. Some ecovillages aim at preserving and strengthening their traditional sustainability (mostly in Latin America, Africa, and Asia), while others are pioneering a new whole-systems approach that addresses the social, ecological, and spiritual dimensions of human living.

A beautiful example of one of these communities, which I know very well, is Hummingbird Ranch in New Mexico. They work with the principle of co-creation. "We celebrate a unique culture in our community as we incorporate the principles and practices of co-creation."

The Co-Creators Handbook, which is written by co-founders Carolyn Anderson and Katharine Roske, is foundational to the development of our community (*www.hummingbirdcommunity.org*)

Their website explains:

> Co-creation is co-participating consciously with the laws or patterns of the Creator; conscious alignment with the essence of self, others and nature. A conscious co-creator is one who surrenders and aligns their will with the intention of Creation, the universal mind, the designing intelligence, Spirit; one who shares their gifts and actualizes their dreams in synergistic play with other co-creators to bring forth a new world.[30]

LOCAL EXCHANGE OR COMMUNITY CURRENCY NETWORK

The second worldwide network that I want to address is the Local Exchange or Community Currency Network, which has some wonderful initiatives that really bring people together. They create a possibility for us to begin to be of service and productive in our communities, without needing any cash to start. People can just start to offer their services and make use of all services offered by the local network. Similar networks have been started all over the planet. A form of community currency is issued at the local level for use in local participating businesses. Go to the database of the Complementary Currency Resource Center, *www.complementarycurrency.org*, to see where all these initiatives are happening.

Community or Complementary Currency Systems such as LETS (Local Exchange Trading Systems) and Time Banks provide an alternative to using official money that is controlled by governments and banks. Local and community currencies:

- are resilient against recession and collapse
- tend to support localization and sharing rather than un-sustainable growth
- prefer local goods and services over globalized production
- can be used for economic and social development

I want to share with two such examples with you. The first is Time Banking, which was started in Washington, DC, by Edgar Cahn, author of *No More Throw-Away People*. Here's some information from their website, *www.timebanks.org*:

> *Time Banks Weave Community One Hour at a Time.* For every hour you spend doing something for someone in your community, you earn one Time Dollar. Then you have a Time Dollar to spend on having someone do something for you. It's that simple. Yet it also has profound effects. Time Banks change neighborhoods and whole communities. Time Banking is a social change movement in 22 countries and six continents.

> *Creating Social Change with Time Banking.* Time Banking can change the world we live in by changing the way the public sector addresses the deep social problems our society still

faces. Children, minorities in poverty, and the elderly are especially hard hit. In these and other areas of social need, Time Banking offers a powerful new approach for social and systems change.

The second example is BerkShares, which is a local currency designed for the Berkshire region of Massachusetts. Dubbed a "great economic experiment" by the *New York Times*, BerkShares are a tool for community empowerment, enabling merchants and consumers to plant the seeds for an alternative economic future for their communities. Launched in the fall of 2006, BerkShares had a robust initiation. Over one million BerkShares were circulated in the first nine months, and over 2.7 million by July 2011; more than 400 businesses have signed up to accept the currency. Five different banks have partnered with BerkShares, with a total of thirteen branch offices now serving as exchange stations. You can read more at *www.berkshares.org*.

THE BASIC INCOME NETWORK (BIEN)

The third worldwide network I want to explore is BIEN, the Basic Income Earth Network. I want to speak about two examples: Former Brazilian President Lula started an initiative in 2003 to close the poverty gap and German Götz Werner, founder of dm-drogerie markt (*www.dm-drogeriemarkt.de*) has been promoting the idea of a basic, unconditional income for each German for years.

Brazil is the first country in the world that has passed a law addressing basic income. Senator Eduardo Matarazzo Suplicy, who worked tirelessly for its implementation, said, "If we really want to eradicate absolute poverty, provide dignity and freedom to all, and build a civilized and just society, a common-sense solution would be to institute a basic income."[31] In October 2003, then Brazilian President Luiz Inácio Lula da Silva launched the conditional cash transfer program *Bolsa Família* as a means of eradicating abject poverty. All families with a monthly income of less than R$120 per capita (implying a situation of poverty) and dependent children under 15 years of age are eligible for the program. In order to receive the cash transfer, families must demonstrate that their children who are younger than 6 years of age have been vaccinated. Furthermore, children between ages 6 and 16 must attend school at least 85 percent of the time. Parents, whenever possible, should attend literacy or professional courses. This program helped 21 million people out of poverty. The new president, as of January 2011, Dilma Rousseff, has vowed to complete the job.

Germany has a strong basic income movement, with dozens of active groups, media attention in newspapers and TV talk shows, and lectures and discussions throughout the country. Within the major political parties in Germany, there are groups and individuals that publicly support a basic income. More than 50,000 German citizens had signed an electronic petition to the German Parliament calling for the introduction of a basic income as of October 2010; see website in note.[32] Götz Werner said in his article "A Basic Income, A Basis for the Future,"

> Is it necessary for our society to allow anyone to fall through the social safety net? Our productivity is constantly increasing but we no longer notice the fact. Owing to our system of paid work accompanied by the imposition of high taxes and other levies, labor is becoming too expensive for many companies, so they are streamlining their operations and moving jobs abroad. However, the unemployed also receive an income, which is financed by taxes, levies, and non-wage contributions. Everyone loses out, and personal incomes and basic benefits are going down all the time.
>
> This could be changed by introducing an unconditional basic income. . . . This would enable individuals to engage in activities as free citizens without worrying about their livelihood and, at the same time, to do work they find sensible and rewarding. They would do work of their own choice for one other, and do so in social security and dignity. . . .
> The basic income would create freedom of action: it would be possible to finance many community and cultural tasks, and many new initiatives would be launched. Many people would rediscover the sense and importance of their work,

for no one would be prevented from working to supplement their unconditional basic income. The difference would be that they would no longer be forced to work.[33]

All these initiatives in community-building, alternative currencies, and basic income come from people who care. This should give us all hope. Many of these movements do not receive widespread media coverage, but they are crucial to know about if we want to resolve the economic and financial issues we are faced with.

CHAPTER 7

TRUE STABILITY AND FREEDOM

What is needed in order to stabilize our economic and our financial worlds?

1. Both worlds need to be regulated by the living reality of the Earth and by our experience of living as a world community. Money can become a "kind person" that serves, instead of an enemy of ours. Money can find its place in the service of care and it can be disciplined by care.
2. Money and economics need no longer be controlled by the God of Money. That means we take a stand for what we want and use money in ways we are all happy with—ways to use money that truly support our well-being and the well-being of the Earth.
3. The caring approach needs to be increasingly ready to come forward in our economic and our financial lives. Through the reemergence of caring, the God of Money in us can slowly die. This death stops the illusion that we find happiness by pursuing money without pursuing care.

We have created a world in which we often think that making money and becoming rich is our road to happiness. To acquire money and live in financial abundance can be beautiful when it is fully heart-based. The differences among us in our financial and material wealth are natural, and do not need to be destructive, as long as we are caring for one another and willing to share. However, it is different when we create excessive wealth which comes from greed and which happens at the expense of others. Good stewardship of money and business can create so much positive energy in the world. There is an interesting website, *www. consciouscapitalism.org*, where you can read more about how adopting a different attitude within day to day business can change everything for good. It is a change of heart in economics and business that creates a better world. (Read more at the end of Chapter 13.)

As Lynne Twist so aptly demonstrates in her book *The Soul of Money*, there is great wisdom in knowing when we have enough and can experience both simplicity and abundance.

To make a well-deserved profit is fair, but too often we pursue that profit (money) at the expense of other things and our focus becomes one of greed. We will address this topic much more deeply in later chapters when we discuss the current collapse of the investment banking system in the United States and elsewhere (see Chapter 12).

I feel that one of the most important areas for attention and rethinking our economic system is regarding the policies and practices for acquiring our homes. This system needs to become much more human and caring. We need to be careful with our focus on making too much profit in the housing sector. When rent and house prices become too high, too many of us end up struggling with monthly mortgage or rent payments, forcing us to have to work too hard to keep our homes.

We haven't found our freedom yet, because we have not created it for each other. In our current financial and economic worlds, we often lose the connection with ourselves, each other, and our planet. This is the result of a money first application over a care first application. *When we apply overall care for ourselves, each other and our planet, we create a new freedom firmly grounded in love.* That freedom comes when we make the gift available to all, spiritualize our material world, and turn it into a sacred world, as many tribal cultures have done and still do. Gratitude for all that has been given to us in the material world is a part of that sacred experience.

We move toward this freedom in the heart when we make the well-being of our planet and its inhabitants the focus of all economic and financial actions. You might say: "This is obvious; what else are economics and finance for?" But it needs to be said, because so much of our economic and financial world is disconnected from the basics of life and is not focused on that well-being. *Our financial world and quite a bit of economic activity have gone off on a tangent, which is endangering our existence and harming our collective well-being.* The way to repair this is to bring money "back home" and discipline its behavior to be in service to the overall well-being of people and the Earth.

Most of us, as individuals, make money to take care of our basic needs. We work to earn our money, and sometimes we borrow it. *We have not really made a clear, collective, conscious choice about how we want to live in our financial and economic worlds.* We tend to live in a way that says that money is needed to survive and that we need to get it. However positive and creative this process can be, it also creates a lot of pain and trouble.

The core of this problem is that we are out on our own in the desert, looking for water, while we could be standing around a fountain, with more than enough water for all. Instead of asking each person to acquire their part of the gift for himself or herself, we could also receive the gift for us all, share it among us, and acknowledge that we all have an equal right to our share of what is available.

There are, I believe, seven principles that can assist us in creating the world we want:

The first principle: We are free and have the freedom to create what we want.

The second principle: Everything, the whole material world and our talents, is a gift to us.

The third principle: Life is a school that teaches us all. There is a purpose behind all that happens, and within the fabric of life lies a deep support system to assist us with our life's journey.

The fourth principle: Nature is a brilliant guide and can teach us a lot about how to make things work.

The fifth principle: To be in community is the key to our survival, and money matters are all about relationships.

41

The sixth principle: The heart lies at the center of all things. It is the mystery and our home and, of course, produces love.

The seventh principle: The spiritual world always helps us and, in that sense, we are never alone.

On a morning in late June 2009, when the breeze off the Hudson River hinted at the humid weeks to come, a middle-aged gentleman, mustachioed and soft-spoken, entered the United Nations Headquarters on the east side of Manhattan. Later that day, this former Catholic priest, and in 2009 President of the United Nations General Assembly, H. E. Miguel D'Escoto Brockmann, rose and took his place behind that famous granite lectern. He gave the opening address on June 24th of a United Nations conference on the world financial and economic crisis and its impact on development, which took place from June 24th to 26th:

> My dear Presidents, Prime Ministers, Ministers for Foreign Affairs, Excellencies, Mr. Secretary-General, Brothers and Sisters all. We, the representatives of states and governments of the world, are meeting at the United Nations because we are going through a most singular moment in human history when our common future is at stake. We are citizens of different nations, and the same time, we are citizens of the planet; we all have multiple and interdependent relationships with each other.
>
> At this critical moment, we must all join our efforts to prevent the global crisis, with its myriad faces, from turning into a social, environmental, and humanitarian tragedy. The challenges of the various crises are all interconnected and oblige us all, as representatives of the peoples of the Earth, to declare our responsibility one to another, and [declare] that together, with great hope, we will seek inclusive solutions. What better place than this United Nations General Assembly Hall to do so.

First of all, we must overcome an oppressive past and forge a hopeful future. It must be acknowledged that the current economic and financial crisis is the end result of an egotistical and irresponsible way of living, producing, consuming and establishing relationships among ourselves and with nature that involved systematic aggression against Earth and its ecosystems and a profound social imbalance, an analytical expression that masked a perverse global social injustice. In my opinion, we have reached the final frontier. We seem to have reached the end of the road travelled thus far, and if we continue along this way, we could arrive at the same destiny which has already befallen the dinosaurs. Therefore, controls and corrections of the existing model, while undoubtedly necessary, are insufficient in the medium and long term. Their inherent ability to address the global crisis has proven to be weak. Stopping at controls and corrections of the model would demonstrate a cruel lack of social sensitivity, imagination and commitment to the establishment of a just and lasting peace. Egotism and greed cannot be corrected. They must be replaced by solidarity, which obviously implies radical change. If what we really want is a stable and lasting peace, it must be absolutely clear that we must go beyond controls and corrections of the existing model to create something that strives towards a new paradigm of social coexistence.

From this perspective, it is essential to seek what the Earth Charter calls "a sustainable way of life." This implies a shared vision of the values and principles promoting a particular way of inhabiting this world that guarantees the well-being of present and future generations. As great as the danger we all face from the convergence of these various problems is, the opportunity for salvation that the global crisis is helping us or forcing us to discover is even greater. We have built a globalized economy. Now is the time to create globalized policy and ethics based on the many cultural experiences and traditions of our peoples.[34]

Lastly, there is a belief which pertains to the common good of humanity, a belief that comes from spiritual traditions and is affirmed by contemporary cosmologists and astrophysicists, that behind the whole universe, every being, every person, every event and even our current crisis, there is a fundamental energy at work, mysterious and ineffable, which is also known as the nurturing source of all being. We are sure that this nameless energy will also act in this time of chaos to help us and empower us to overcome selfishness and take the action needed so there is no catastrophe, but an opportunity for creating and generating new forms of coexistence, innovative economic models and a higher sense of living and living together.

In conclusion, I would like to place on record my deep conviction that the current scenario is not a tragedy but a crisis. Tragedy has a bad outcome, with an Earth that is damaged, but can continue without us. Crisis purifies us and forces us to grow and find ways to survive that are acceptable for the whole community of life, human beings, and the Earth. The pain we now feel is not the death rattle of a dying man but the pain of a new birth. So far, we have fully exploited material capital, which is finite, and now we have to work with spiritual capital, which is infinite, because we have an infinite capacity to love, to live together as brothers and to penetrate the mysteries of the universe and the human heart.

. . . Care implies a nonaggressive attitude to reality, a loving attitude that repairs past harms and avoids future harms and, at the same time, extends into all areas of individual and social human activity. *If there had been sufficient care, the current financial and economic crisis would not have occurred.*

. . . We will start with the assumption that the community of peoples is simultaneously a community of common goods. These cannot be appropriated privately by anyone and must serve the life of all in present and future generations and the community of other living beings. The common good of humanity and the Earth is characterized by universality and freedom. *All persons, peoples, and the community of life must be universally involved. No one and nothing can be excluded from this global common good.* Furthermore, by its nature, it is freely offered to all and therefore, cannot be bought or sold nor be an object of competition. Moreover, it must be continuously available to all; otherwise the common good would no longer be common. . . . As we all have our origin in the heart of the great red stars where the elements that form us were forged, it is clear that we were born to shine our light and not to suffer. And we will shine our light again—that is my strong expectation—in a planetary civilization which is more respectful of Mother Earth, more inclusive of all people and with more solidarity with the poorest, which is more spiritual and full of reverence for the splendour of the universe and which is much happier.

With these words, our discussions at this very important Conference on the world financial and economic crisis have begun. In providing a context for these issues, I wish to emphasize that we will have to set aside all selfish attitudes if we are to take advantage of the opportunities that the current crisis offers. Such attitudes only seek to preserve a system which seems to benefit a minority and clearly has disastrous consequences for the vast majority of the inhabitants of the planet. We must arm ourselves with SOLIDARITY and COOPERATION in order to make a qualitative leap forward to a future of peace and well-being.[35]

We can only echo this profound statement and explore its ramifications as we shift into a care-first world.

In this first part of the book, we have been looking at a cauldron, a space that can hold us all and care for us, and to which money can return. We can be in the Garden; it is a dream that is real.

WHAT IS THE GARDEN?

In the Garden we stand together
with the presence of love in our hearts.
We are in community and co-create our dreams.
We hold each other, ourselves, and all life on this planet in love's embrace.
We are present with that love and live that love.

We connect heaven and Earth,
work with spirit and matter in their perfect marriage.
We are happy and fulfill our soul's calling.
We serve the greater good,
the evolution of ourselves, each other, and our planet.

In the Garden we are at peace.
We experience the mystery, we are ourselves, and have each other.
In the Garden our souls can rest
in a world of love where justice prevails.
It is the manifestation of our deepest dream.

In the Garden we live that dream.
We do not wait for it to happen.
We put love in action.
We apply care-first.
We create a beautiful world.

In the second part of the book, we will look at the quality of the financial transactions we make, to see how much they actually serve us and our planet; we will explore the foundation of a love-based economy, a new use of money, and more.

A LOVED-BASED ECONOMY

OUR COMMON ILLUSION ABOUT MONEY

What is the illusion about money that the God of Money in us represents and the Prince of Peace in us redeems? We will look in detail at what the different transactions we engage in look like, in the light of community and Earth, and in the light of the real world of goods and services.

When we look at the global casino of currency-trading and stock market manipulations, when we are making money out of money for the sake of money itself, what are we doing? What happens between us? Contrast that with a fair exchange of goods and services given and received. That is real, as is gifting.

I believe that our illusion begins with a sense of ownership about money, rather than an understanding about the stewardship of money—the "me" versus the "we" world. "Money is mine" versus "Money is part of the gift." Shouldn't money itself be a part of the gift we receive and share and steward? Is it not part of what we call our global financial commons? (We will discuss the global financial commons in Chapter 15.) This illusory path starts when we disconnect from a shared space and play the money game without considering the consequences of that game and the well-being of others and the planet. Another part of the illusion is that we can think that playing this game will create happiness, or even that it even serves us at all. Unfortunately, this type of behavior is very prevalent. Look at the collapse of many investment banks in 2008, which has wreaked havoc with much of our financial and economic worlds. There is a piece of this in all of us that needs to come home and give back what it took, share with others, and experience humility.

What also takes us away from ourselves, from each other, and from our planet is confusing money with true wealth, which consists of the gifts we and our planet can offer? Money is only a means to acquire real goods and services. Because the material world is grounded in ownership and money gives us the power to acquire and own things, we tend to only associate money with wealth.

TODAY'S WORLD
Today's world is not the Garden yet.
How do we go there?
We are sharing a dream, a possibility.
What is needed to make it real?
And where are we?

Let's begin with looking at the money world,
what money is in our economy
and how it affects our lives.
Why does it have such a powerful position in our lives?
Why is it true that, in a certain sense, money makes our world go round?

Money is a means of exchange
that is needed for most of what we need for our daily living.
We need it to receive our part of the Earth's gift.
This surely makes it an intimate part of our world.
It gives money a position in which it can have power over us if we allow it to.

Money has a strong relationship to ownership.
When we buy something, it becomes ours
and we legally own the things we purchase.
This makes the money world ownership-based.
This connection to ownership can give money itself a lot of power.

Most of us feel that we need to earn our living and make money.
This tends to be an individual effort, something we do alone.
It is up to us to acquire our piece of the pie, which is not given to us.
We work hard for it and can choose to go into
battle and competition with each other.

An environment like this can foster the forces
of greed, fear, desire for power, possessiveness, and selfishness.
It is also the birthing ground for a money-first attitude,
"We need money first, because then we can have what
we want and have what we need."
We need to have money to have life.

Material well-being doesn't necessarily bring us together.
There is still a lot of aggression and emptiness in well-to-do countries.
So although there is progress, many problems remain.
We will look at how we can build a love-based economy,
give money its rightful place, so that we can finally relax and enjoy our lives.

Our emotions and sentiments in relation to the illusion about money tend to have five aspects: fear, greed, possessiveness, selfishness, and the desire for power. *"When I can lay my hands on that money, then I can have all I want and the world is my oyster. I can create my fortress here and I will be free and happy."*

These negative traits are balanced in us by five aspects that have the power to lift all of us out of that common illusion: caring, sharing, loving, giving, and receiving. *"When I receive the money in my life with gratitude and use it to care for myself, my family, community and the world, I help to create a fair and more balanced world for all."*

We are dealing with a few huge issues in our financial world that we will need to resolve together. It starts with the way money is being created in our world, and it also involves any place where we get lost in the money game for the sake of money itself, in our global casino.

In her book *Beyond Globalization: Shaping a Sustainable Global Economy,* Hazel Henderson writes about the unreal economy, the global casino:

> Finance, which is supposed to serve the world's real production and exchange processes, has largely de-coupled itself from the "bricks and mortar" of real economies of local places and communities. Today's globalised economy has led to a sixteen-fold increase in world trade since World War II. More than 40,000 multinational companies with 25,000 affiliates dominate two-thirds of the global trade. Yet, this large volume of trade accounts for less that 10% of the 24-hour global currency trading of US $4 trillion every day.
>
> This global economy of flows in these market networks is increasingly abstract and divorced from national policy-makers and local affairs, grassroots lives and livelihoods as well as the natural ecosystem. This has triggered new risks and inequalities. These include further marginalization of social groups, indigenous peoples and whole countries such as many in Africa; widening the gap between the rich and the poor and the overall increase of global poverty, as documented in successive editions of the UNDP [United Nations Development Programme] Human Development Reports. Within one generation, according to the Living Planet Index by the World Wildlife Fund for Nature and the New Economics Foundation, around 30% of Nature's productive capacity has been lost.[36]
>
> . . . International financial operations escape national regulations and are centered in London, New York, Tokyo, Hong Kong, Singapore and [in] offshore tax havens such as Switzerland, the Cayman Islands, the British Virgin Islands, Cyprus, Antigua, Liechtenstein, Panama and the Nether-

lands Antilles, the Bahamas, Luxembourg and the Channel Islands. [37] . . . The continual shocks and instabilities in today's global financial markets have finally led to some cautious re-thinking on the part of finance ministers and central bankers on the need for a "new financial architecture." [38]

. . . In our efforts to help oppose injustice, alleviate poverty, and reshape the global economy to serve people, higher standards, human development and Earth's ethics, we are learning that all these efforts begin at home—with ourselves. Former Russian culture minister and Harvard sociologist Pitirim Sorokin in his last book, *The Ways and Power of Love* (1953), quoted French paleontologost/theologian Pierre Teilhard de Chardin, "when humans discover the power of love, it will prove more important than the harnessing of fire." [39]

We've gone off on a tangent. It is all a matter of returning back home to ourselves. Home is always where the heart is. In the next chapter, we will look more closely at the love-based economy, which is a true foundation for economics. Living from the heart in our economic and financial worlds is naturally sustainable or, to say it more strongly, it is the only choice we have to establish a new foundation for economics and a healthy financial world.

Below is the logo of our Scottish charitable company, World Finance Initiative, which we created in 1996 to start exploring the connection between money and the heart.

Figure 8.1 The logo of the World Finance Initiative.

Our world economy is ready for a new heart.

Every time money is being used to care, we form this heart.
This circulates a new energy through the organism of our economic system, creating
a healthy and sustainable world in which the well-being of people
and our planet Earth are ensured.
We call this healing flow of transformed finance golden water. In our logo, you see a
Greek goddess pouring this water into our world system.

The aim of the World Finance Initiative is to create a love-based economy
and a care-first world.
We define care-first as all actions in which money is being used to care.
We define money-first as pursuing money at the expense
of the well-being of people and the Earth,
at the expense of our caring, our values, and our passions.

Whenever we work for money at the expense of ourselves,
each other, and our planet Earth,
everything suffers.
Every time money and care are separated, we create more pain in the system.
When we put care-first in all our actions and use money in service of this,
we and our planet Earth shine.

It is a simple truth.
Applying it puts so much of today's economics back in order.
Taking it to its furthest consequence, it can save the planet.

CHAPTER 9

SIMPLICITY AND THE HEALING OF OUR FINANCIAL WORLD

To connect love to economics or money may seem a contradictory act for many of us. The word *love* is also not always understood that well. I experience love as fundamental to all of creation. It lies at the core of our lives and learning processes and therefore also at the core of our economic and financial lives. The fact that love is not always present in our financial world makes it even more imperative to bring love in.

THE SIGNIFICANCE OF LOVE

A love-based economy and a love-based use of money can open up a whole new path for humanity. Of course, as people, we can struggle with love. We can associate it with a kind of emotional love, which isn't necessarily real love. Love, which can be the foundation for finance and for our economies, is a core experience of the self.

I have felt my whole life that love, not fear, is foundational in all people, and that love resides at the heart of our universe. This is a personal experience, but I am sure many others share this with me. I experience love as "the substance of our Universe." This substance is an all-pervasive field of energy that guides all we do and all that we are.

When we witness the horrific things that we as people can do, it can be hard to believe that love would be guiding all this from some point within creation, from a caring consciousness. I feel we each need to decide for ourselves whether we believe this to be true or not. It is an intimate matter.

It is my experience in the field of finance and economics that, without question, love is the key to solving the problems at hand. Whether we translate love itself into caring, sharing, loving, giving, and receiving doesn't really matter. What matters is that these five qualities are love and that we, as human beings, find that love in our own hearts, among ourselves, for the Earth, and toward the source of all things.

When we feel fear, or the contraction that comes from fear, we are not breathing into love. In a fear-based economy and with a fear-based use of money, many of us experience this. From this point of fear, it is hard to see the abundance of money and the abundance of life, and often want to control our lives and our financial situation. Maybe we are afraid we will lose out. Maybe we do not sense the caring support that life itself can give us, when we open ourselves to it. That support can come our way as if an angel says to us, "Rest in me and all will be well." As if the angel says to all humanity, "You will make things better for yourself, for others and for your planet, when you follow the language of your heart."

In *Dare to Care* I am speaking openly about love as a real option for life and as a true foundation for finance and economics. Maybe not everyone will agree with my experience and some people will see it differently, but I can only be myself, open and honest. I feel that love matters and is crucial to the survival of our species.

I want to introduce the concept of overall care and compassion as a starting point for governing our planet. I hope that we can each find our unique contribution, learn to work together, be in council, and organize life on our planet accordingly. Let us connect the dots and see that love has the power to not just elevate relationships—which is the main realm in which we refer to love—but that it can do the same in all directions and in all aspects of our culture. My body knows this to be true. I pray that we can fully express who are and that we will work together to achieve our vision. We are not dreaming when we think of a better world. We see reality, we see a possibility. Let's explore a beautiful world together, totally grounded in real life, totally grounded in common sense, good business practices and legislation, government policy and local decision-making. Let's create a beautiful world where it matters, where the heart matters.

A love-based foundation for finance and economics can be built by us all. Hazel Henderson coined the phrase "the love economy" in the 1960s, describing an economy of the heart, an economy of unpaid and voluntary work. Let's add "the love-based economy" and "the love-based use of money" to this, where love guides every aspect and creates a new foundation for finance and economics for generations to come.

LOVE AND ECONOMICS

I have found that connecting love to economics,
using love as the point of reference for assessing all economic actions,
is the most fundamental thing we can do.
I see love as the substance of our universe.

My background is in counseling, assisting people with what is going on
deep inside of themselves in relation to their manifested lives.
In that process of self-healing,
I find that love is always the point of reference.

With every pain we have, conflict we experience, with every disharmony in our lives,
we always seek to return to a center of love, our core,
and every time we come home there,
we find peace and all is in order.

For me, this is exactly the same way with economics.
In 1989, I began to look at issues
we all have with money, survival, and work.
I was always looking at our well-being in those areas.

In looking for answers to these issues
I started building a vision
for a love-based economy,
a care-first world
And a Garden state on Earth.

I define a care-first world as a world
where money is serving the well-being of people and the Earth
and is not used at the expense of that well-being.
I define a love-based economy as an economic system
with love and caring as its motivators,
with sharing at its heart and giving and receiving as its flow.

I define the Garden state on Earth
as a place of happiness and joy, togetherness and peace,
where we are all well-fed, housed, educated, and healthy
and Nature has been brought back to its natural abundance
with its ecosystems restored.

Having now lived and worked with this vision
for nearly fourteen years,
I find that it provides me and others with a solid foundation
for what the economics of our future can look like
in every detailed aspect.

THE TRANSFORMATION OF FINANCE

In 1993, I had an inner vision where I was shown that one day
I would start a charitable organization called World Finance Initiative,
whose aim would be to help to stop war, hunger, and pollution
by using finance in a different way.
I thought to myself, what can this different way be?

Two years later in the middle of the night
I was shown money
and I saw the presence of love
moving inside of the money,
through which they merged and became one.

The next morning I was thinking
about money being imbued by love and I wondered
what happens when this kind of money is used in a bank?

How will the bank respond to people's financial needs and problems,
when love becomes the motivating force behind its use of money?

This experience took me into a level of consciousness that was easy to experience,
but not so easy to understand: perceiving money itself as an expression of love.
The logo of the World Finance Initiative is a Greek goddess
pouring golden water out of a blue pot over the Earth.
This golden water symbolizes money as love and care, healing our world.

I began to speak
about the transformation of money itself.
Of course money is just a thing
and what makes a difference with money and how we experience it,
is how it is being used.

When someone makes a financial contribution to support you and your work,
that money is imbued with the love and care the person feels for you
and the money feels great.
When a greedy landlord takes too much money from you, the money is imbued
with greed
and that money doesn't feel good.

So money becomes what we do with it.
Therefore money as love or money as care
is something we create.
Money can become a beautiful tool for creating a caring world.
It can also be a tool for creating a cold and unhappy world.

We can connect its use to
our love, our care, our desire to share, to give, and to receive.
We can connect its use
to our greed, our fear, selfishness, possessiveness, and our desire to have power.
We can create our use of money as we see fit.

SIMPLICITY

We all want to make the best use of our strengths, talents, and gifts.
We all need our home.
We all need our sustenance.
We all need health care.

We all share the Earth and receive its gifts.
We can steward these gifts together.
We all have an equal right to food, shelter, education, and health care.
We all need to have enough.

This is a fundamental entitlement for all.
When this is not happening we can experience it as not just, not fair, and not
equal.
In order to establish, it we need to reconsider how we look at work, money,
and our government policies, which are all tools for its provision.

Work can become the contribution we each want to make,
where we do what is needed and share our unique gifts.
Money can become a constructive force supporting us all.
It can be seen as a gift from the Earth, as all material things are.

Money can become the expression
of our caring, sharing, loving, giving, and receiving heart.
How can it flow in our world,
so that we establish this simple picture of care, fairness, and sustenance for all?

First of all, we need to make sure that all products and services are supporting
our well-being and the well-being of the Earth.
Then we need to implement a fair and mutually supportive
exchange mechanism of products, services, and finance.
All our transactions need to be moved by love and care and be based on sharing.

They all can serve the greater good and build positive relationships
and not serve our greed, fear, possessiveness, selfishness, and desire for power.

The same applies for all transactions made in
stock markets, in currency trading,
in the investment and mortgage business, and in our banks.

We can see how we redistribute money so that all are empowered to give
their best and receive their rightful entitlement.
This vision needs to be held and implemented.
This vision is simple.

CHAPTER 10

TWELVE QUESTIONS TO ASK ABOUT A FINANCIAL TRANSACTION

In early 2010, I created a series of twelve questions we can ask ourselves in relation to any financial transaction we make. They help us to investigate our behavior and motivation in relation to our daily transactions and look at the quality of each transaction.

1. Was the transaction I just made moved by love and care?
2. Was that transaction based on sharing?
3. Was the transaction fair and mutually supportive?
4. Was the transaction human?
5. Was there contact with the other party?
6. Did it build positive relationship?
7. How did the transaction affect the Whole?
8. Could its effect have been better?
9. Did you have a good experience of money in this transaction?
10. What did this exercise teach you and where did it leave you?
11. Would you call this a constructive transaction?
12. What would need to happen for it to be completely constructive?

There are some examples of how to use the questions in Table 10.1, 10.2, and 10.3.

Example 1: Paying the monthly rent. Table 10.1 explores some of the issues around paying the monthly rent.

1	Was the transaction I just made moved by love and care?	Yes, I do appreciate our landlord and am grateful for our home.
2	Was that transaction based on sharing?	Hard to say. It is just business.
3	Was the transaction fair and mutually supportive?	To a certain degree, but it is too expensive.
4	Was the transaction human?	No, I just transfer the money online.
5	Was there contact with the other party?	No.
6	Did it build positive relationship?	Yes, in the sense that I pay on time and they do take care of us.
7	How did the transaction affect the Whole?	Hard to tell. It still creates too much tension.
8	Could its effect have been better?	Yes.
9	Did you have a good experience with money in this transaction?	More or less.
10	What did this exercise teach you and where did it leave you?	Frustrated with how we live together. Would like more sharing and care.
11	Would you call this a constructive transaction?	No.
12	What would need to happen for it to be completely constructive?	A fairer rent and more contact.

Table 10.1 Questions and Answers about Paying the Rent

I always say, as do many others, that money is relationship. One of the main results of **people taking our workshop is that they realize**

they can put their heart and soul into the transactions they make and become more conscious of the quality of each transaction. This can look like a lot of work, but it definitely pays off. I do realize, however, that whatever positive changes we can make individually in the quality of our transactions, *we will not have arrived in the new land until we collectively have brought that positivity into all our financial transactions and created a monetary system we can support with all our heart.*

Example 2: A bank clerk issued a loan at the bank's interest rate and moved the money into the customer's account. Table 10.2 explores the issues around a bank clerk's issuing a loan.

1	Was the transaction I just made moved by love and care?	Not really. I just work here; it's my job I need to make money. I feel quite indifferent about it.
2	Was that transaction based on sharing?	In a sense yes, we want to help the customers.
3	Was the transaction fair and mutually supportive?	Not totally; the interest is a bit high. I think it would help the people more if there was no interest or a very low one. It definitely supported us, but how it was for the client, I am not sure.
4	Was the transaction human?	Yes, it was between people.
5	Was there contact with the other party?	I didn't see the customer. In this case I just completed the deal.
6	Did it build positive relationship?	I hope so.
7	How did the transaction affect the Whole?	In a positive and negative way.
8	Could its effect have been better?	Yes. We could do it differently so that it serves the customer more.
9	Did you have a good experience with money in this transaction?	Yes, it is a good communication tool and can support us all.

10	What did this exercise teach you and where did it leave you?	It was painful. I realized how numb I am. I just work for money. I would like to have more meaning in my life. I would like to make my money doing something that I love. I feel too lonely and separated from the world in this job.
11	Would you call this a constructive transaction?	No.
12	What would need to happen for it to become completely constructive?	I need to stand behind myself more and what I do. Decide whether I want to do this job and if I do, see how I can help the Bank to be more serving towards its customers and think a bit less of their own advantages.

Table 10.2 Questions and Answers about Making a Bank Loan

Many people work too hard for their money and are not able to fully express their real gifts. In our workshop, one of the main themes is to get people to look for their real gifts and find a way for money to support that. We have created a world where the job market is too oriented toward the commercial world and not enough toward facilitating everyone exploring and using their most natural gifts. In order for us to be able to have that full expression and do the work we love, we need to create more of a support system. This is very much a matter of intention. We can decide that we are going to support all people to make their unique contributions towards our world community. When we all set this intention, the steps that are needed will follow, and we can slowly accomplish our goal.

Example 3: Someone made a gift after attending "Meeting the Mystery of Money" workshop. Table 10.3 explores the feelings of a person who made a donation after attending a workshop.

| 1 | Was the transaction I just made moved by love and care? | Absolutely; perhaps the most conscious transaction I have ever made. |
| 2 | Was that transaction based on sharing? | Yes. You shared your time and energy to help me grow. I share the money so you can live well. |

3	Was the transaction fair and mutually supportive?	Yes. Would have liked to give more as the value of the weekend is more, but this is the limit of what I can afford at the moment.
4	Was the transaction human?	Yes. It was handed personally.
5	Was there contact with the other party?	Yes. I looked you all in the eyes.
6	Did it build positive relationship?	Yes.
7	How did the transaction affect the Whole?	It was a love-based transaction.
8	Could its effect have been better?	Not as far as I can see.
9	Did you have a good experience with money in this transaction?	Yes.
10	What did this exercise teach you and where did it leave you?	It made me relive the transaction and brings me to a space of love.
11	Would you call this a constructive transaction?	Yes.
12	What would need to happen for it to be completely constructive?	It already is.

Table 10.3 Questions and Answers about a Gift Given After Attending a "Meeting the Mystery of Money Workshop"

The answers in Table 10.3 came from a real participant. In the workshop, people decide on the financial contribution they want to make at its end. We always say to them: "Let your heart speak, be considerate of your own situation and of ours, and know that this is our livelihood."

We do not have a fixed charge, although we can give people some idea, if they need that. The workshop really helps people to connect to their hearts in relationship to money. Near the end of the workshop, almost everyone is ready to make a heartfelt gift in gratitude for the self-wisdom and new perspective they have gained from their participation.

We, as the facilitators and hosts, go through beautiful experiences. People really give of their time, wisdom, and financial support. They appreciate the work and us, and we deeply relate to one another. When I compare this experience at the end of the workshop with what most people express around money at the beginning of the workshop, it is the difference between living in hell and existing in heaven.

CHAPTER 11

OUR MONEY SYSTEM AND ITS NEED FOR RESTRUCTURING

At the start of our workshop "Meeting the Mystery of Money," we begin by exploring our deepest money issues. It is always very moving to listen to everyone's experiences, which are shared with such honesty and in such depth. Two of the main themes that are expressed in every workshop we've done are the experience of the unfairness of the money system in relation to the inequalities of income and money distribution among us all and the experience of a deep lack of social support.

Every time we start the workshop, I feel that what people are describing is their version of a living hell. Yet people are simply and honestly sharing their own experiences. By the end of the workshop, all this has completely changed, which doesn't mean that we have resolved our issues, but we have definitely gotten a much better grasp of them. My question is: "What is the relationship between this hell we experience and the structure of our present money system?"

In the workshop, I speak about the resurrection we must all go through in relation to the death and rebirth of the God of Money in ourselves and our culture. This renaissance is the shift away from fear, greed, selfishness, possessiveness, and the desire for power and towards caring, sharing, loving, giving, and receiving. How is this transition related to our present money system, to how money is created and to how we use it in our world community?

There is video called *The Money Fix,* produced by Alan Rosenblith, edited by Hazel Henderson, and distributed by Ethical Markets TV, which gives a detailed description of how our debt-based system was created. You can watch it on *www.ethicalmarkets.tv* (video 0333). Here are a few pertinent quotes from this very informative video.

> Conventional money is not created by the government, as many people believe, and is not even created by the central banks, although they are part of it. It is actually created by the banking system.
>
> . . . People see these films about the US mint and the government printing office and they see sheets of dollars being run off the printing presses. So they think it is the government that's printing the money, but this is not the real source of money. The real source is banks.
>
> . . . The Federal Reserve is a private institution owned by commercial banks, who are members of the Federal Reserve system, which includes all nationally chartered banks.
>
> In 1910, a group of top American bankers met on Georgia's Jeckyll Island to discuss ways of stabilizing the country's banking system. Congress passed the Federal Reserve Act in 1913, giving this private corporation a monopoly over issuing the nation's money supply. How then did the power to issue something as fundamental as money fall into private hands?
>
> . . . For every new dollar created in the monetary system, you have a corresponding debt. That works both for the Federal Reserve dollars themselves and for the bank deposit dollars that are based on them.
>
> The private banking system literally creates our money out of nothing and runs it into the economy. The only way in which new money can get into the economy and, ultimately, in your pocket, is via a bank loan. This means that every dollar you have ever seen is someone's debt to a bank.

The catch is that they want more repaid than what they have given [you].

When you go to a bank and you borrow $100,000 to buy a house, they will check whether you are a good credit [risk] and they will decide to create the money by entering it electronically into your account and say "You have to bring back $200,000 in the next 20 years." The $100,000 of the first loan is created. The second one [second $100,000], the interest rate, is not created. That is how the money is kept scarce. So they send you into the world, to compete with everyone else to bring in the second $100,000. It is competition between different players for interest that is not created. So there is always less money than is necessary. . . . We are competing with each other for an inadequate supply. There will never be enough money to repay banks.

. . . So our experience of money being scarce is an artifact of the money system. In a properly run monetary system, there will be no scarcity of money.

. . . Competition does have its place in urging us to our highest level of performance and fulfillment. But health is dependent on cooperation. We don't have the liver competing with the heart for blood and for nutrients. There is this inherent cooperation that leads to the health of the entire entity.

. . . There isn't any profit motive in natural systems.

. . . There is, without a doubt, a mega crisis that we are facing in the coming years and the big elephant in the living room is the money problem and, unfortunately, most people who are active in the sustainability movement and environmental movement don't understand the nature of this problem and we are not going to make any significant headway with sustainability or restoration of the environment until we solve the money problem.

. . . What we are doing is really reinventing the exchange process. We need to mediate exchanges in a different way than we have done before. The debt money system creates money on the basis of interest-bearing debt. It is not debt itself that is at fault, it is the interest component that is attached to the debt.

I do not have an issue with interest as a fair service fee for taking out a loan. It is only when it gets out of hand and creates too much stress for the borrower that it becomes a problem.

MONEY, FINANCIAL INSTITUTIONS, AND FINANCIAL INSTRUMENTS

In the next section of this chapter, my friend and colleague Ernie Robson addresses the question "What is money?" and looks at the nature of financial institutions and financial instruments. Ernie holds degrees from Yale and the Sloan School at the Massachusetts Institute of Technology (Bachelor of Science in Administrative Science and Master's degree in Management). He worked for the US government in the Office of Management and Budget, a part of the executive office of the president of the United States under Presidents Ford and Carter, from September 1976 to August 1980. In this capacity, he dramatically increased the resources available for enforcement and for better research and development at the US Environmental Protection Agency. Ernie helped create and teach training courses on the US federal budget process for the US Office of Personnel Management through the EOP Foundation. Ernie is an entrepreneur and problem-solver by nature, having helped start more than a dozen small businesses, from high tech to medical services. He is currently working on a project to increase the amounts of certified organic and non-GMO soybeans and grains available in the international commodities markets. Ernie asked to help Louis with this book because he believes that it is time for caring people to take back responsibility for money and power in the world.

Traditional definitions of money always mention that money is a medium of exchange and a store of value. It has also recently been called "information" by economist Hazel Henderson and others.[40] Many think of money as "the root of all evil." This is a common misinterpretation of the Christian Bible. The original quote is that "Love of money is the root of all evil" (1 Timothy 6:10).

The misinterpretation continues in the New Testament (Luke 6:20):

"Blessed are you poor, for yours is the kingdom of God."[41] It turns out that this is a partial quote of something that has nothing to do with money, but rather with the experience of knowing the kingdom of heaven within.[42] Christ was most likely describing an inner state of being, and not admonishing us to become poor or stay poor as the path to heaven. These erroneous scriptural interpretations have caused all manner of misunderstanding in the Christian world. Spiritual and good-hearted people of the world have essentially abdicated responsibility for money and financial and tax policy to those who are less interested in helping others and putting care first. We can see the results all around us.

In the United States, we have seen, for the first time, a great separation of the wealthy from the middle class. Two-worker families are the norm, leading to a breakdown in family life, and for the first time in our history, most adult children are doing less well financially than their parents.[43] Our safety net "welfare" system has created a lack of dignity and a permanent disincentive for a father to stay with his wife and children. Unfortunately, when a person on welfare tries to work and earn an income, his or her standard of living actually goes down.[44] The system also costs an enormous amount to administer and police.

Our taxation system also needs wholesale reform. It is incredibly complex and costs a great deal to administer and interpret.[45] Yet the tax burden on the rich has lessened, while most Americans have higher taxes than ever (if you combine federal and state income taxes, social security taxes, Medicare deductions and property and sales taxes).[46] The enormous and illegal shadow economy of drugs and of other criminal behavior goes untaxed, costing taxpayers an additional several hundred billion dollars a year.[47]

As a means of exchange, humans have used all sorts of things for money, from cowry shells to gold coins to multicolored pieces of paper. Don't laugh about the shells! They were used as money in Africa, China, India, and North America for thousands of years![48] As a store of value, humans found that certain products and services did not keep well when stored or hidden away and buried. When these goods and services were converted to money (shells, gold, paper) they, in general, maintained their value, but not always! In post-World War I Germany, paper money became so worthless that people needed to take a wheelbarrow of it to buy a loaf of bread.

If, in the overall economy or in specific markets, the money supply grows more rapidly than the growth of real goods and services, price inflation is the result. This is what occurred in the housing market for the years leading up to the worldwide crisis of 2008. The interrelationship of goods, services, and money is a subject about which many hundreds of books have been written. What is fascinating is that the only constant truth about money is that money is what we collectively agree that it is. But every time we get stuck on a definition, something changes and the definition is obsolete! The most enduring truth is that money is what we agree that it is, and we need to change our agreement to reflect our dramatically changed world.

On a larger, society-wide scale, we have collectively created many financial institutions (for example, banks, insurance companies, stock markets, and futures markets). We have populated these institutions with many thousands of financial instruments. Some instruments are relatively simple, like a credit/debit card, and some are a bit more complex, like stocks or bonds. Some are so complex that almost no one really understands them. Witness the shock of the leaders of the world's financial institutions when they realized that the "derivatives" their traders had created, which seemed above the iron rules of the marketplace, were not. All of these institutions and many of the financial instruments were created to manage and spread risk. And in general, many have great value. For example, the commodities markets seem to the outsider to be wildly speculative. However, the market as a whole is credited with lowering the costs of most foodstuffs by about 10 percent. For more information, read note. [49]

Another truth about money, financial institutions, and financial instruments is that while they can be incredibly useful and valuable in society, they are also subject to the abuse of individuals and individual companies. This is why we as a society created regulations and regulatory bodies to check the worst of abuses. But clearly, over the last two decades, these regulatory institutions were systematically undermined by government officials of both parties in the United States. The government in turn was driven by the leaders of these regulated institutions. Billions of lobbying dollars were in part responsible for deregulation. In addition, and perhaps worse, there is a revolving door of key jobs in government financial agencies. These jobs are filled by a small interconnected group of financial leaders, academic leaders, and government officials. This is a unique situation in the world of government regulation. For example, in environmental regulation, this situation, which can cause one-sided decision-making, would be a great cause for alarm. Unfortunately, most normal citizens and our representatives have awarded near-priesthood status to these leaders in the financial world.

Leading up to the recent financial crisis, what most people, even the insiders, underestimated was how closely interlocked our financial institutions had become through the use of derivatives. These arcane and complex financial instruments further broke down any prior regulatory body and law. When you can make a risky home mortgage look like a safe bond, pay rating agencies to rubber-stamp this illusion, and even bet against the safety of those supposedly safe bonds, the system is primed for fraud and abuse. Some details of what this lead to are discussed in the next chapter.

Perhaps the most sociopathic behavior was that of those insiders who created and clearly understood the risks of the system. They used it to engineer a massive shift of trillions of dollars from middle-class homeowners and taxpayers to the wealthy. Historians will look back at the decade from 2000 to 2010 as the most massive bank heist in history. And, as shown in the Academy Award- winning documentary film *Inside Job*, it was indeed an inside job.[50]

Clearly, we cannot abdicate responsibility for the money system and its institutions and instruments, leaving its administration and oversight to those motivated by greed and selfishness. They have severely damaged our world. They have left our global financial commons in a highly toxic and polluted state. We clearly need re-regulation of financial institutions and instruments, but we need to go way beyond that. The bigger picture is that an enormous brain drain happened during some of the greatest global crises imaginable. The best minds—the engineers, scientists, mathematicians, and lawyers—had their intelligence and energy diverted into causing the greatest financial disaster in history. It is time that we as citizens end this diversion of our best and brightest, and instead focus these great resources on solving our clear and potentially species-ending global problems in the areas of energy, ecology, health care, and international relations. We cannot leave this up to those who said "Trust us!" We did that before, and we see the results.

We need to fix our money system, and the taxation and welfare and innovation systems we have now. But we need to start with our money system. It is privately held in the hands of a wealthy few and their priesthood of academics, managers, and government regulators. This needs to be changed. And, as we discuss in chapters ahead, even the basis for money needs changing. We have created or allowed others to create the current system. We can undo it and create something better—indeed we must.

THE WEB OF DEBT

I watched a video of Ellen Brown's on her website, *www.webofdebt.com*.[51] She wrote *The Web of Debt,* in which she shows very clearly what has gone wrong with our present money system and how it affects our lives, but she also shows what we can do to put it right. In her video she says:

> Hello. my name is Ellen Brown. I am an attorney and author of eleven books. My latest book is called *The Web of Debt: The Shocking Truth About Our Money System and How We Can Break Free.* The shocking truth about our money system is that there is no real money in it, except for coins, which compose only one ten-thousandth of our money supply.
>
> All our money is created privately by banks when they make loans. This includes Federal Reserve notes or dollar bills, which are issued by the Federal Reserve, a privately owned central bank, then lent to the US government and to other banks. Banks are allowed to leverage their capital base into many times that sum in loans, covering the outgoing checks from their deposit pool; and that is where all of our money comes from.
>
> The bankers are in control of the money supply. When the banking system falters or when we have a credit freeze like we have right now, our entire economy falters, because our entire economy is based on money that is issued as

credit by banks. The result has been that businesses can't get the money that they used to be able to get, so they wind up laying people off, which creates unemployment. The housing market is collapsing because we do not have the credit we used to have. States are going bankrupt because of this and because they do not have the tax base they used to have. Because of unemployment, they do not have as much income to tax and because of the housing problem, they don't receive enough taxes on housing either.

Forty-eight out of fifty states are currently not able to meet their budgets, either this year [2011] or next year. What they are doing instead is that they are having to slash services. This is at a time when we particularly need social services, because people are out of work. They are raising taxes again at a time when people can't afford higher taxes, because they are out of work or having trouble finding work.

On top of this, we are selling off our state resources. These are things we actually paid for and now we have to rent them back. These are roads, bridges, parking meters, airports and ports, which they are selling off to private investors, and we end up paying fees for our own assets. During the Great Depression of the 1930s, the problem was that there was not enough money in the system. The food was there; the food was lying on the ground; but there was no money to pay the workers to gather it, and no money to buy it in the grocery stores. So the food was there and the people were starving. What was missing was the flow of money or the flow of credit to get the food to the people.

We can set up an alternative credit system in which states would own their own banks. Any large public entity can own its own bank. A municipality or a state university system, like the University of California, can own its own bank. One state in the Union, North Dakota, already does this. North Dakota is one of only two states that are currently able to meet their budgets. In fact, the state now has the largest surplus it has ever had. It has plenty of money for everything it needs to do. Plenty of money for student loans. It makes low-interest loans to farmers. It funds municipal bonds. It acts as a sort of central bank in the state and partners with the other banks, so they do not feel threatened. They are actually helped by the whole system. The people managed to keep their money within their own state. The bank was founded in 1919, when the farmers were losing their farms to the Wall Street bankers (a similar situation to what we have now). They got fed up with this and passed legislation by which all the state's revenues went into the state-owned bank of North Dakota. These revenues created a huge deposit base, which they can use, as any bank can, to create loans for all their credit needs. Every state could and should do this. In California, we are now 26 billion dollars in the red and therefore we are having to take all these extraordinary measures to try to meet our budget. What we could do is use our state revenues and leverage them into credit for the state. The state has 17 billion dollars on deposit in banks, most of them out-of-state banks; and it has hundreds of billions in pension funds and rainy-day funds. It could leverage some of this money into credit that could basically solve our credit crisis. We could fund infrastructure and all those things we think we do not have the money for, because money is only credit. We could create the credit for those things if we set up our own banking system. This is my proposed solution to the banking crisis, and if you have any questions you can go to my website, *www.webofdebt.com.*

CHAPTER 12

THE COLLAPSE OF THE BANKS IN THE UNITED STATES: THE PERFECT STORM

I have always felt that the current mortgage system is questionable and sometimes very uncaring. I have found that this concern is shared with countless others. The financial troubles we have gone through highlight the flaws in the current way we organize finances and the economies of the world.

In the rest of this chapter, Ernie Robson explains about the contributing factors to the perfect financial storm.

Let's start by trying to understand Collateralized Debt Obligations (CDOs), the complex financial instruments that were the most immediate cause of the current economic crisis. Then we will briefly look at the contributing factors that led to the near meltdown of our global financial system, and what needs to be done about it.

What is a CDO? And how can something that most of us are not familiar with contribute so strongly to the collapse of the United States Investment Banks in 2008?

Rudimentary forms of CDOs have been in use for decades, but only in limited situations. The financing subsidiaries of American automobile companies used to package auto loans and then sell them or finance them in the larger debt markets. CDOs, in the form of bonds, were also used for decades in the United States at Fannie Mae (FNMA, the Federal National Mortgage Association), Ginnie Mae (GNMA, the Government National Mortgage Association), and Freddie Mac (FHLMC, the Federal Home Loan Mortgage Association).[52] In discussing CDOs, Wikipedia says:

> ... The first CDO was issued in 1987 by bankers at now-defunct Drexel Burnham Lambert Inc. for Imperial Savings Association.
> ... CDOs offered returns that were sometimes 2-3 percentage points higher than corporate bonds with the same credit rating.
> ... This made U.S. CDOs backed by mortgages a relatively more attractive investment versus say U.S. treasury bonds or other low-yielding, safe investments.
> ... A decade later, CDOs emerged as the fastest growing sector of the asset-backed synthetic securities market. This growth ... reflect[ed] the increasing appeal of CDOs for a growing number of asset managers and investors, which now include[ed] insurance companies, mutual fund companies, unit trusts, investment trusts, commercial banks, investment banks, pension fund managers, private banking organizations, other CDOs and structured investment vehicles."[53]

By mid 2005, the sales of CDOs were major revenue sources for investment banks, and rating these CDOs had become a major profit center for the bond rating agencies. With the large amounts of money in international capital pools looking for a safe investment with a higher return in the early 2000s, the CDOs backed by mortgages in American homes seemed a good bet. Unfortunately, no one was looking too hard at the values and riskiness of the underlying mortgages backing the CDOs. As the US housing market prices rose higher and higher, larger loans were given to fewer and fewer credit-worthy buyers, so the subsequent large default rates for the mortgages underlying the CDOs became the cause of widespread reduction in the value of CDOs. This widespread "markdown" of CDO values led to the elimination of the small reserves for loss carried at many investment banks and insurance companies.

Let's look at what happened with the collapse of the banks. Like the Great Depression of 1930s, the 2007–2008 economic meltdown was a perfect storm. For a more detailed discussion of parallels with the Great Depression, see note.[54]

First, it needs to be understood that a massive amount of the world's surplus cash was poured into all of the developed countries' housing markets from 1990 through 2007. Thus, underlying the US housing market bubble was a world bubble. In all developed nations, a housing credit bubble grew. This was created by cash-rich nations like China and the Middle East oil countries investing heavily in that most basic of human assets, the home.

But the US economy was special for many reasons. First, the dollar was the reserve or base currency for the world. The United States was also the biggest and most sophisticated financial market in the world, and it was interconnected to the major financial markets of all other countries. So, while the bubble burst all over the world, it was the United States that was the epicenter of "the perfect storm."

From the late 1990s on, the US government, under both Presidents Clinton and Bush, had been creating incentives and pressure to make home-owning more possible. This led to more risky lending practices, encouraged by the US government. Simultaneously, in 2000, the US federal and state governments decided that they were not going to regulate the derivatives market, so US local banks and mortgage-originating companies started issuing high-risk mortgages at very low interest rates.

The investment banks on Wall Street started to collect these cheap and not too secure mortgages and packaged them up into bonds called mortgage-backed securities (MBSs). These bonds were then the basis for another layer of bonds representing the value, interest, and principal payments of the mortgages.

These were called Collateralized Debt Obligations (CDOs), and they were not real assets. They were derivatives, in which the money flow is "derived" from the assets. There was a rapid widespread adoption of CDOs insured by companies like AIG as a high-return, lower-risk financial instrument.

The credit rating agencies would stamp these bonds with a very good rating of AAA, even though a lot of the mortgages underlying these CDOs were very risky. CDOs were then sold all over the world. And because of the high rate of interest for a seemingly safer investment, they could be sold, for example, to a municipality in Norway that needed some more money for its budget or pension fund investments. The Norwegians would hear about these good bonds that had a great interest rate from a Wall Street firm and buy them.

The local banks and, more importantly, the mortgage-originating companies, knew that people had started defaulting on their mortgages. However, because they could then pass off these higher risk mortgages to be packaged and resold with very little due diligence on the value of the underlying mortgages, they kept passing more and more of them to Wall Street.[55]

Then, as it became clearer that many people might default and actually were defaulting on their mortgages, the investment banks bought other derivatives called *credit default swaps,* or CDSs, from insurance companies like AIG [American International Group]. These CDSs were a way of hedging the CDOs' financial risk by betting that, should homeowner who took out the mortgage default, investors would still make money from the insurance. In many cases these CDOs were sold with very little due diligence and very little disclosure of underlying risks. Remember, these derivatives were all, by statute, exempt from financial regulation. The financial institutions responsible could all get away with it, with no rules or regulatory oversight of the rules. In addition, when the ultimate crash began to be perceived by market makers like Goldman Sachs, these companies began heavily buying another type of derivative that was created as a hedge that both CDOs and their risk-reducing CDSs were going to fail.

Goldman and others like Morgan Stanley were making money by packaging and reselling mortgages. At the same time, they were betting against the financial soundness of the CDOs by purchasing massive amounts of derivatives that were bets against the mortgage market. For this behavior, selling something they knew was flawed, they are now being sued by some of their former clients. In essence, they were making a great deal of money selling what they knew to be a faulty product, while at the same time (for nearly 2 years in advance of the collapse) making massive profits from the ultimate failure of CDOs. One hedge fund run by John Paulson, working closely with Goldman, made over 12 billion dollars betting against the CDOs that Goldman and others were selling.

Many consider this fraudulent, although, to date, under current laws it is difficult to bring any fraud charges to any court for these, at the very least, highly immoral activities. And the rewards were huge. For more information, read note.[56] Ultimately, we must look at who gained and who lost and hold them accountable for any windfall.

In summary, a completely unregulated derivative industry in essence created a vast supply of money for home-buying. This was the proximate cause of the bubble in US housing prices. Thus, the recipe for disaster was complete. Individuals were given more and more money to chase the same number of homes. This created a 40 percent increase in home prices and mortgages that would ultimately prove too expensive to bear. As more homeowners couldn't pay their mortgages, both the principal and the interest, the CDO bondholders started losing their money, because the value of the bonds dropped and they were not receiving their interest.

The collapse started with Bear Stearns investment bank, which [had] created two hedge funds (for rich individuals who wanted to make higher-risk investments). They were buying the CDOs at a time that CDOs were losing value and they had a hard time selling them. For more information, read note.[57]

As a result of this perfect storm, Bear Stearns led the failure of ten other major financial institutions, which happened in the course of just a few weeks. Additionally, hedge funds collapsed, General Motor's financing arm GMAC (which had gotten into mortgages too) collapsed, and Freddie Mac, Ginnie Mae, and Fannie Mae all imploded.

Major world Investors wanted assurances that they would get their money back. And, in the case of major investors like China and the Middle East oil countries, the US government could absolutely not afford to have them be afraid to invest in the US financial markets. A departure of these cash-rich nations from the US government securities market could have actually led to the collapse of the world's financial markets. The bailout that followed was done to save these investment banks but, more importantly, to preserve the world financial system from a total meltdown.

In the process, some institutions like Lehman Brothers and many others could not be saved.

Of great concern for the longer term, a new phrase was coined for the institutions that were bailed out. It was said they were "too big to be allowed to fail." Given that these were all private institutions (although many, like AIG, [are] now majority-owned by the US government), this is a highly disturbing turn of events, and clearly sets the agenda for reform of the world's monetary systems.

In the US, a bipartisan commission with strong investigatory powers was established and began to dig into the causes of this near-complete meltdown. Their questions and conclusions were reported by the US Financial Crisis Inquiry Commission [FCIC] in January of 2011 in *the Financial Crisis Inquiry Report (Cosimo Reports, 2011). They asked:* How did it come to pass that in 2008 our nation was forced to choose between two stark and painful alternatives—either risk the collapse of our financial system and economy or commit trillions of taxpayer dollars to rescue major corporations and our financial markets, while millions of Americans still lost their jobs, their savings, and their homes?

The commission concluded that this crisis was avoidable. It found widespread failures in financial regulation; dramatic breakdowns in corporate governance; excessive borrowing and risk-taking by households and Wall Street; policymakers who were ill prepared for the crisis; and systemic breaches in accountability and ethics at all levels (see *www.fcic.gov/report/conclusions*).

In response to the crisis and after many congressional hearings, the US Congress enacted the Dodd–Frank Wall Street Reform and Consumer Protection Act (Pubic Law 111–203,[58] H.R. 4173). It was signed into law by President Barack Obama[59] on July 21, 2010. For more information, read note.[60]

Thus the US government's response to the 2007 financial crisis was the granting of emergency financial powers by Congress to the US executive branch and the US Federal Reserve in 2008 by the Emergency Economic Stabilization Act of 2008 (H.R, 1424)[61] with its TARP or Troubled Asset Relief Program (signed into law in October 2008), and the longer-term 2010 Dodd–Frank reforms.

Although this response to the financial crisis was the most significant piece of financial regulation and reform since the Great Depression in the 1920s and 1930s, it seems it was only the beginning. The legislation was progress but, in the eyes of many economists, the reform went nowhere near far enough. The legislation clearly was not a fundamental change, as is actually needed.

Massive problems remain to be solved. The jury is still out on whether the United States has accomplished anything more than papering over the problems in the US and world financial systems. Further reforms are needed, but exactly what is needed will remain to be seen. In the short run, these reforms bring some hope of financial stability, but it is clear that the underlying problems remain.

However, the United States does get credit for an attempt to begin to restore regulatory control over the global financial commons. In 1970s, environmental protection laws were created in the United States to protect our environmental commons. This was the beginning of the end to the selfish and greedy behavior of pollution. Today in the global financial commons, there is a clear need for a new legal framework that better defines what financial practices are unacceptable. And there is also the need for severe penalties and joint and several liability for violators of these rules of behavior. (See note[62] to read about the similarities between financial and environmental regulation.) Although deregulation can sometimes make sense and contribute to consumer well-being, this is simply not true for the financial commons. The financial meltdown of the US money system is clearly a lesson that teaches us what happens when we sacrifice common sense on the altar of deregulation! The recent global crisis was a wake-up call that we need to re-establish what money is and how it is used. It was the perfect storm of many things that could and did go wrong with money, financial instruments, financial institutions, regulatory agencies and government decisions. Politicians and world leaders from all walks of life and all countries have agreed it is time to rethink our global financial commons.

CARE-FIRST BANKING AND BUSINESS

The following are a number of living examples of what is already happening in the shift toward sustainability, the application of care-first, and the transformation of our financial systems.

TRIODOS BANK

Triodos Bank N.V. is a bank based in the Netherlands with branches in Belgium, Germany, the United Kingdom, and Spain. It is a pioneer in ethical banking. Triodos Bank finances companies that it thinks add cultural value and benefit both people and the environment. The name, Triodos —*tri hodos*—is translated from the Greek as "three-way approach." Triodos has an active international department, supporting microfinance initiatives across the developing world. Here are some quotes that reveal the philosophy of the bank's chairman of the Board of Management, Peter Blom, which appeared in *two articles in Triodos Magazine*. The first is from the article "Sustaining Sustainability" (Summer 2008):

> Financial success is of secondary interest for Peter Blom, Chairman of the Board of Management, when he reflects on an eventful year. For him, the changes in how we relate to each other and the earth and the virtuous cycle between

them are much more exciting. Peter Blom believes money exists to serve us:

"Profit is not an objective in itself. It's a yardstick. It shows that you are working efficiently but says nothing about the content of what you are doing. We, on the other hand, start with the content of an activity and focus on its sustainability. The first thing we consider is 'How can this contribute to sustainability?' Then, as bankers, we ask ourselves 'Is it viable?' If our judgment is correct, profit should follow automatically." Peter Blom recognizes that this is a radical departure from conventional business. It means reappraising the role of money and its place in the economy.[63]

The next quote is from "A Bank That Connects People" (March 2009):

While the financial world collapsed last year [2008], Triodos Bank remained as solid as ever. In fact, as billions of pounds were wiped from the balance sheets of some of the world's best-known banking names, Triodos actually grew by 25%. Chairman of the Executive Board Peter Blom puts this down to a growing movement of individuals and organizations who demand more from their bank. Peter Blom is entirely open about the key to Triodos Bank's success.

... "A bank needs to make connections. First and foremost is the relationship it creates between savers and borrowers. We also have 'shareholders'—in our case depository receipt holders—but the bank doesn't only serve their interests. Our bank is structured specifically to avoid that situation. But it's important to establish connections with nature, our fellow human beings, and the problems facing us all. You need to ask yourself—'what do we need to do now to achieve the transformation for the future?'"

... "Beginning last year [2008], individuals in the Netherlands have been able to open a current account with Triodos Bank. We aim to offer a complete package of services, so that people can transfer all their banking to us. It is already possible in the Netherlands and [we] hope, eventually, to offer the same services to customers in the UK, Belgium, and Spain and at a new branch we plan to open in Germany later this year [2009]. For a long time saving with a sustainable bank was something you 'did on the side.' Today, people want to be able to opt for a different kind of bank for their day to day banking as well. And this growing interest in sustainable banking has gained momentum as a result of the financial crisis."[64]

THE GLOBAL ALLIANCE FOR BANKING ON VALUES

The Global Alliance for Banking on Values (*www.gabv.org*) originally consisted of eleven banks that joined together to form a new alliance in a move to build a positive alternative to the current crisis in the global financial system. As of July 2011 there are thirteen member banks. This new partnership plans to develop new ways of building organizations that are better suited to long-term sustainable thinking, and also wants to develop new forms of ownership and economic cooperation. The alliance was launched at an event held in the Netherlands from March 2–4, 2009. The then eleven-member alliance was founded by the Bangladesh Rural Advancement Committee (BRAC) Bank; ShoreBank Corporation, a United States-based community development and environment bank; and Triodos Bank in the Netherlands. Other member banks of the alliance as of 2011 include Alternative Bank ABS in Switzerland; Banca Popolare Etica in Italy; Banex, Banco del Exito in Nicaragua; BancoSol in Bolivia; Cultura Bank in Norway; the GLS Bank in Germany; Merkur Cooperative Bank in Denmark; Mibanco, Banco de la Microempresa in Peru; New Resource Bank in the United States; OnePacificCoast Bank in the United States; Vancity in Canada; and the XacBank in Mongolia.

The member banks, with assets worth over US $10 billion and serving over seven million customers in twenty countries, came together for their first meeting during the March 2009 event. Given the current financial crisis and its profound influence on the global economy, the members believed that the timing of the alliance's launch was crucial.

Speaking at the launch, Mr. Peter Blom, the CEO of Triodos Bank, described the leaders of the eleven member banks as "forces of change" who stuck to simple, core banking services that balance "people, planet, and profit." He noted the fact that these banks were still profitable and crisis-resistant, unlike their mainstream contemporaries, and stated that the leaders of these eleven banks held some of the solutions to the global financial crisis (story reported on *www.microcapital.org*).

Ms. Mary Houghton, President of the ShoreBank Corporation in 2009, stated that the establishment of such an alliance was very important, given the current crisis and the need for a healthier, more sustainable economy. Ms. Houghton said the alliance would focus on promoting responsible finance, supporting existing banks in this regard, and also helping develop new ones.

Speaking at the event, Her Royal Highness Princess Máxima of the Netherlands called for banks to "go back to [the] basics" and follow the traditional banking activity of acting as an intermediary between the saver and the borrower, in addition to building a strong relationship with customers. She also stressed on the need for banks to thoroughly assess how much each customer could really handle as a loan (story reported and posted by Bharathi Ram on *www.microcapital.org*).

THE GRAMEEN BANK AND THE MICROCREDIT MOVEMENT

The Grameen Bank is a microfinance organization and community development bank started in Bangladesh that makes small loans (known as microcredit or "grameencredit") to the impoverished without requiring collateral. The name Grameen is derived from the word *gram* which means "rural" or "village" in the Bengali language.[65] The following quotes are from the Grameen Bank website, *www.grameeninfo.org/index.php*:

> In 1974, Professor Muhammad Yunus, a Bangladeshi econo-mist from Chittagong University, led his students on a field trip to a poor village [in Bangladesh]. They interviewed a

woman who made bamboo stools and learned that she had to borrow the equivalent of 15p [U.S. $0.22] to buy raw bamboo for each stool she made. After repaying the middleman, sometimes at rates as high as 10% a week, she was left with a penny profit margin. Had she been able to borrow at more advantageous rates, she would have been able to amass an economic cushion and raise herself above subsistence level.

Realizing that there must be something terribly wrong with the economics he was teaching, Yunus took matters into his own hands, and from his own pocket lent the equivalent of £17 [$27] to £42 [$66] to basket-weavers. He found that it was possible with this tiny amount not only to help them survive, but also to create the spark of personal initiative and enterprise necessary to pull themselves out of poverty.

Against the advice of banks and government, Yunus carried on giving out "micro-loans," and in 1983 formed the Grameen Bank, meaning "village bank," founded on principles of trust and solidarity. In Bangladesh today [2011], Grameen has 2,564 branches, with 19,800 staff serving 8.29 million borrowers in 81,367 villages. On any working day, Grameen collects an average of $1.5 million in weekly installments. Of the borrowers, 97% are women and over 97% of the loans are paid back, a recovery rate higher than any other banking system. Grameen methods are applied in projects in 58 countries, including the US, Canada, France, the Netherlands, and Norway.[66]

Professor Yunus and Grameen Bank received a Nobel Peace Prize in 2006 for "their efforts to create economic and social development from below." He said,

October 13, 2006 was the happiest day for Bangladesh. It was a great moment for the whole nation. An announcement came on that day that Grameen Bank and I had received the 2006 Nobel Peace Prize. It was a sudden explosion of pride and joy for every Bangladeshi. All Bangladeshis felt as if each of them received the Nobel Peace Prize. We were happy that the world has given recognition through this prize that poverty is a threat to peace. Grameen Bank, and the concept and methodology of micro-credit that it has elaborated through its 30 years of work, have contributed to enhancing the chances of peace by reducing poverty. Bangladesh is happy that it could contribute to the world a concept and an institution which can help bring peace to the world.[67]

ARRASATE OR MONDRAGÓN COOPERATIVE CORPORATION

Arrasate or Mondragón (Basque and Spanish official names; Mondragoe is an unofficial Basque name) is a town and municipality in Gipuzkoa province, in the Basque region of Spain. Its population on 31 December 2007 was 22,112. It is known mainly as the place of origin of the Mondragón Cooperative Corporation (MCC), the world's largest worker cooperative, whose foundation was inspired in the 1940s by Father José María Arizmendiarrieta. The MCC was started in 1956.[68] In 2002, the MCC contributed 3.7 percent towards the total GDP of the Basque region and 7.6 percent to the industrial GDP. The valley of the High Deba where it is located enjoyed a high level of employment in the 1980s while the rest of the Basque industrial areas suffered from the steel crisis.[69]

Noted poverty expert and sociology professor Barbara J. Peters of Southampton College, Long Island University, has studied the incorporated and entirely resident-owned Basque town of Mondragón, Spain. "In Mondragón, I saw no signs of poverty. I saw no signs of extreme wealth," Peters said. "I saw people looking out for each other. ... It's a caring form of capitalism."[70]

According to Wikipedia, the Mondragón Corporation is a federation of worker cooperatives; its origin is linked to the activity of a modest technical college and a small workshop producing paraffin heaters. As of 2010, it was the seventh-largest Spanish company in terms of turnover and was the leading business group in the Basque country. At the end of 2009, it was providing employment for 85,066 people working in 256 companies in four areas of activity: finance, industry, retail, and knowledge. The Mondragón Cooperatives operate in accordance with a business model based on people and the sovereignty of labor, which has made it possible to develop highly participative companies rooted in solidarity, with a strong social dimension, without neglecting business excellence. The Cooperatives are owned by their worker members and power is based on the principle of one person, one vote.

A quote from the book, *We Build the Road as We Travel, Mondragón, a Cooperative Social System* by Roy Morrison, says:

> The Mondragón Cooperatives in the Basque region of Spain, at more than fifty years of age, remain the world's outstanding example of building a cooperative social system within the context of a now global market economy. This effort is foremost an adventure. It's an expression of individual and collective energies and dreams, as well as the requisite careful business practice of tens of thousands of co-operators engaged as social entrepreneurs.
>
> What's most exciting, for me about the Mondragón co-operatives is their daily wrestling with the dynamic tension between freedom and community—between the needs, rights and imperatives of the individual and the similar, and often conflicting, imperatives of the group. Mondragón 's greatest social innovation and contribution has been the understanding, developed through hard work, sometimes troubling experience, and innovative practice, that freedom and community are fundamentally interdependent and indivisible. You cannot have true freedom without community; you cannot have true community without freedom.[71]

EMPLOYEE OWNERSHIP

Employee ownership occurs when a business is owned in whole or in part by its employees. Employees are often given a share of the business after a certain length of employment, or they can buy shares at any time. They also often have boards of directors elected directly by the employees. Some corporations make formal arrangements for employee participation, called employee stock ownership plans (ESOPs).[72] The individual employee owners in an ESOP company directly benefit when their company succeeds. Thus ESOPs are unique in that no one has a stronger interest in the quality of their products and the total satisfaction of their customers than the employee owners of an ESOP company. By far the most common form of employee ownership in the United States is the ESOP. Almost unknown until 1974, about 11,000 companies now have these plans, covering over thirteen million employees.

CONSCIOUS BUSINESS OR CONSCIOUS CAPITALISM

There are presently many companies that have become great examples of what happens when we care for the products and services produced and the environment, and we care for all stakeholders—employees, customers, suppliers, and investors/shareholders. A new term for this is *Conscious Business* or *Conscious Capitalism,* clearly all applications of care-first. A few of these examples are InterfaceFLOR, Google, Whole Food Markets, Southwest Airlines, Starbucks, and Tata from India. Patricia Aburdene writes about the trends in her book, *Megatrends 2010: The Rise of Conscious Capitalism,* published in 2007.[73] As described in Wikipedia:

> *Conscious Business* is a term used to describe a business enterprise that seeks to be aware of the effects of its actions, and to consciously affect human beings and the environment in a beneficial way. Conscious Business also refers to a movement towards "values-based" economic value, where values represent social and environmental concerns globally as well as locally. The Conscious Business movement has emerged from the theory of Corporate Social Responsibility, and is currently related to movements such as the Not Just For Profit Business Models, Conscious Consumerism, and Socially Responsible Investing. Conscious Business

could also be referred to as *Conscious Capitalism*. As well as being a category of business, it can also mean an individual and personal approach to business, as in "she did business consciously."[74]

As described on the Conscious Capitalism Institute website (*www. cc-institute.com/cci*), Conscious Businesses are built on three core principles:

Deeper Purpose: A Conscious Business has a higher purpose that transcends profit maximization. It is clear about and focused on fulfilling that higher purpose, which evolves dynamically over time.

Stakeholder Orientation: A Conscious Business focuses on delivering value to all of its stakeholders and works to align and harmonize the interests of customers, employees, partners, industry participants, investors, the community, and the environment to the greatest extent possible.

Conscious Leadership: In a Conscious Business, management embodies conscious leadership and fosters it throughout the organization. Conscious leaders serve as stewards to the company's deeper purpose and its stakeholders, focusing on fulfilling the company's purpose, delivering value to its stakeholders, and facilitating a harmony of interests, rather than on personal gain and self-aggrandizement.[75]

Below are some quotes from John Mackey, CEO of Whole Foods Market and cofounder of FLOW (Freedom Lights Our World; *www. flowdealism.org*), from his 2006 article, "Conscious Capitalism—Creating a New Paradigm for Business"[76]:

Do we need a new way to think about business, corporations, and capitalism for the 21st century? Do we need to create a new business paradigm? Corporations are probably the most influential institutions in the world today and yet many people do not believe that they can be trusted. Instead corporations are widely perceived as greedy, selfish, exploitative, uncaring—and interested only in maximizing profits. In the early years of the 21st century, major ethical lapses on the part of big business came to light, including scandals at Enron, Arthur Anderson, Tyco, the New York Stock Exchange, WorldCom, Mutual Funds, and AIG. These scandals have all contributed to a growing distrust of business and further eroded public trust in large corporations in the United States.

. . . We can remove most the hostility toward business and capitalism if we change the way we think about it. Business needs to become holistic and integral with deeper, more comprehensive purposes. Corporations must rethink why they exist. If business owners/entrepreneurs begin to view their business as a complex and evolving interdependent system and manage their business more consciously for the well-being of all their major stakeholders while fulfilling their highest business purpose, then I believe that we would begin to see the hostility towards capitalism and business disappear.

In summation, business is fundamentally a community of people working together to create value for other people, their customers, employees, investors, and the greater society. Business interacts within a harmony of interests.

CHAPTER 14

A NEW WAY FOR MONEY

In 1996, we started our charity, World Finance Initiative; we lived high up in Scotland in the wild and pure countryside, which felt like living on the moon. The impulse of the World Finance Initiative is to share the understanding that *we, as humanity, have the freedom to regulate the flow of money according to our deepest wishes and heart's desire and that there is no need to accept the mess we are in; that, together, we can find the clarity to heal the financial world at its heart and that this is the same as the healing of our own heart. The healing of our own heart will give us the clarity to direct money in this new way. The way of the heart is fully applicable in business.*

In paying our employees, we can express our appreciation for the work they have done and for who they are. In paying our suppliers, we can show gratitude for their service, and give support and care for their business. When our customers appreciate our business because we provide quality and care for them, they gladly pay us. We can all be happy when fair profits are being made. Then we can add well-deserved value above cost, by which we can be supported in our livelihood. When the financial exchanges among people are fair and mutually supportive, it is a win-win situation for all. It is caring and supportive. It is real togetherness and sharing.

As long as we are not overcome by stress and fear and the desire for power, have not fallen into the trap of thinking about ourselves all the time (selfishness), and are not chasing money without caring about others and the Earth (greed and possessiveness), this comes quite naturally to us all, doesn't it?

Our heart is a powerful tool and the home of our true nature. It is not always easy to be in our hearts as we all have had disappointments in life, have experienced hurtful situations, and we might find it hard to open up again. However, deep down, I feel we are all looking for that love in life and we do not need to be ashamed of it, nor pretend it isn't so.

A NEW WAY OF USING MONEY

I describe golden water as a flow of money moved by love and care, as transformed money, healing us, healing the life on our planet, and healing our financial world.

It took long to prepare and was slowly prepared by the heart. A lot of pain had to be cleared for this idea to arrive and for us to be ready. It can be applied in all financial transactions, in all dealings with money, in all financial procedures and regulations. The idea is very simple, practical and not difficult to apply.

There are five principles to a new way of seeing and using money:

- *The first principle* is that money serves everything it comes in contact with and therefore enhances its well-being.
- *The second principle* is that money can be a container for, or carrier of, the energies of caring, sharing, loving, giving, and receiving. I visualize these energies as a five pointed-star that can lift all humanity and the whole material Earth. This is the key to everything and replaces the energies of fear, greed, selfishness, possessiveness, and the desire for power. Money is the container or carrier that affects everything around it in all directions; it will either be a constructive or destructive force.
- *The third principle* relates to our intention, to the way in which we direct the flow of money. It is how we think and feel. It is what we consciously decide. It is how we want to create our world, our life on Earth.
- *The fourth principle* is about the Golden Water. It is the concept that money supports all, that it is a part of an abundant universe that is shared by all and cared for by all. Money is in our midst as a great communicator of value, of what we hold precious in life. It expresses quality, achievement, a service well done, and all that is good in us, and rewards us accordingly. It carries all business

transactions that are fair and mutually supportive. It is
a part of all profit that comes from good actions, good
business, and right relationship.

- *The fifth principle* is about our relationship to each other
  as a world community; it is an agreement we create as a
  world community about how we decide to use money on
  our planet and how we communally learn to apply these
  five principles.

How can we use money as a tool to empower ourselves? We cannot be
productive when we are hungry; without health care, education, or a
proper home; when we are suffering from inhumane, stressful work; or
when we are not fully expressing ourselves. *To be supported in these areas is
an investment, not a cost.* As long as we are supported by either basic income
or real job opportunities and are empowered by them, it helps move
everyone forward.

The key is allowing money to empower us. A transaction with money
can either empower or disempower us. When we give money to someone
or to an organization that uses it in a constructive manner, we will feel
satisfied with having made that gift. When we give money and it isn't
used well or honored, we may regret our action, because we realize that it
did not empower the recipient. We all need to take responsibility for our
choices and do our share. *When we support each other financially, that action
should empower us to become more of who we are.*

*How can we create a world where we all can make our unique contributions
and use the talents and gifts we have been endowed with and be supported to
do so?* I have shared with you real-life examples of how we can more
constructively live our economic and financial lives (see chapters 6, 13, and
20). I know that there are many people with jobs who are really happy and
work for companies they love, people who can express their best and who
are supported when they do so. At the same time, we all know that for a
large segment of our population this is not happening, not to mention all
the people who have no work, no home, and who go hungry.

Proposals to create certain levels of guaranteed income can change
this. At the same time, we want to live our lives creatively in our businesses,
in the arts, and in our various professions. A guaranteed income provides

us with a place to start. It handles our survival needs, because the basics of life are provided for; then we can look at what we really want to do in life. The choices can run the gamut from volunteering to creating a business. The possibility of a basic or guaranteed income is clearly a subject that leads to a lot of discussion. These discussions have been going on in Germany for many years. I welcome this, because it is of great importance to resolve these issues together. I also want to stimulate that discussion among us on our online platform. This subject clearly requires more in-depth conversation and clearer understanding. German businessman Götz Werner has some very interesting points of view on this.[77]

We need to find the positive balance between taking initiative and caring for one another, between private ownership and sharing, and between competition and cooperation. In the end, it will be, once again, a combination of the wisdom of the heart and our common sense that will offer us the practical answers and solutions we need. It will come from the balance between the head and the heart. I believe that to help us find better answers, we need to study the global commons and experience our financial world as a part of the global commons. We will explore this more fully in the next chapter.

In the second part of this book, we have explored our present money system and how we can move in a new direction, based on creating the foundation of love for both economics and finance.

WHAT IS A LOVE-BASED ECONOMY?

A love-based economy is an economy
where caring, sharing, loving, giving and receiving
are the forces motivating our behavior;
where in our dealings with money, goods, and services
we are in an experience of love.

We receive the gifts of our material Earth,
we are grateful for them, we feel loved by life;
loved by the giving and sharing forces
of Nature, of our Creator,
of our heavenly Father and Mother Earth.

100

We share those gifts; we care for each other with them.
We do not take from each other, possess the gifts,
or use ownership to have power over others.
We make sure that everyone has enough
and we steward the planet's gifts together.

When someone works for us or does us a service and we pay them,
the payment is an expression of our gratitude and appreciation;
it is how we honor that person.
When we have a company we aim to work together and share.
We use money to love.

In a love-based economy our work has meaning.
We make our specific contribution to the whole;
we share the unique gifts we have and follow our inner calling.
We play our part in the orchestra and harmonize with others playing their parts.
Our work is always in service of each other, ourselves, and our planet.

When we get up in the morning and go to work, are we in an experience of love?
When we are at work and making money, are we experiencing love?
When the answer is yes, we live in a love-based economy.
When it is no, this economy is not a part of us and we can ask ourselves why.
That is how simple it all is.

We can create our lives.
We have the power within.
We have the power to create what we dream.
When our work is what we dream of, we are in an experience of love.

PART THREE
A CARE-FIRST WORLD

CHAPTER 15

OUR GLOBAL FINANCIAL COMMONS

In old English law, the common (or commons) was a tract of ground shared by residents of a village, but belonging to no one. It might be grazing grounds, or an open area like the village square, but it was property held in common for the good of all. Global commons is that which no one person or state may own or control and which is central to life. [78] For more information, see note.[79]

The term global village has become popular to suggest that the entire world's population belongs to the same community. Related to this idea is the management of the earth's atmosphere as a global commons (see note for more information about this).[80]

From here we can move toward the concept of a financial commons. I made my connection with Hazel Henderson by signing a "Transforming Finance Statement," which I found on her website, *Ethical Markets* (*www. ethicalmarkets.com*)[81]. It states that the signers, from the European Union, China, India, Australia, Brazil, Canada, and the USA agree that:

> Unbridled greed-driven speculation, the improper use of public infrastructure technology for activities such as high-frequency trading, together with a misguided self-regulatory ideology, reduced system resilience, damaged the financial commons and the trust on which we all depend.

The Transforming Finance group outlined necessary principles and conditions to operate the shared global financial architecture, consistent with 21st-century realities, as discussed in the same statement:

> The Committee on Transforming Finance, a multinational network of career market participants: investors, asset managers, business executives, philanthropists, academics and financial authors, holds that the financial system is a global commons and calls for a new set of rules that would allow it to be governed in full conformance with this reality.
>
> We, as beneficiaries and active participants in capital markets, affirm our responsibility to reform them from within, so that all those still-voiceless stakeholders who are now excluded and exploited can be heard and their communities appropriately served. If we are to avoid future systemic failures in the global financial system, we must re-think the underlying design flaws that precipitated the financial crises. We must move beyond Bretton Woods[82], where this financial commons was first defined within a set of global rules and institutions in 1945, as well as beyond recent attempts at reforms that have not addressed fundamental questions, including:
>
> - What is the purpose of finance in human societies?
> - What human values and principles should guide finance and its institutions?
> - What are the limits of markets, money-based trading, and transacting within the global commons?
> - How can finance serve equitable, ecologically sustainable governance of the global commons (climate, biodiversity, oceans, atmosphere, and space) while reducing inequality, respecting human rights and acknowledging non-market-based, traditional societies?[83] ...

Figure 15.1 The Transforming Finance Logo.

I feel that we need to make a fundamental change in the way we look at money. When I had my experience in 1987 of envisioning that the whole material world is a gift to us all, it was a deepening experience of our global commons. Is money a part of the global commons, or can it be? To me money is an already an inherent part of it, because it is a way of tracking our transactions with goods and services, which are all part of the gifts we receive.

It is very important to come from a new mind-set, to have a different starting point from which we look at our financial and economic issues and at the steps we need to take, individually and collectively. Let's look inside that mind-set. Maybe we should call it a heart-set or a soul-set or a body-set or a spirit-set. This different vantage point starts with gratitude for the gifts of life, for all that we can share and care for. It starts with the responsibility we carry for this beautiful planet,—which looks like heaven on Earth in so many places—for ourselves, and for all living creatures on it. It starts with a full heart and a relaxed and serving brain, filled with true care for ourselves, for each other, and for the Earth.

When we start with care-first, we can heal all the wounds we've created with our behavior around money and create a world we all love to live in and can be proud to pass on to the next generation. It is important that we create a world that does not invite a money-first attitude by the way we organize our money, work, and survival system. We have the capacity to create a money, work, and survival mechanism we can all be fully satisfied with. I believe we can reach that common ground among us.

What has been so fascinating in doing the workshop over the years is that everyone seems to agree on the vision we share and we all seem to carry similar issues, which resolve themselves in a similar fashion. Maybe part of the mystery around money is that money is such a huge common denominator for us all; therefore, it is possible that the really clear, workable answers can work for us all. Let's put on our thinking caps, with big hearts in our heads, and see how we can resolve this together.

I would like to share some material from a wonderful website called *Share The World's Resources* (*www.stwr.org*). Its executive director, Rajesh Makwana, wrote an article in 2006 called "Global Commons—Our Shared Resources." It is an overview of the issues surrounding the global commons, in relation to globalization, economic justice and the need to create a more sustainable world:

> The subtle monopolisation of the global commons began in the middle ages when the rights to land were claimed by the aristocracy and feudalism was commonplace. The common people and their resources were thus exploited by those who owned the land. Over time, this accumulation of power through resource acquisition, allowed cities to plunder the country, taking control of yet more land and resources and thereby establishing ever larger empires. This plunder was enforced through an ever expanding military force.
>
> The same principle of monopolisation currently threatens countless resources, common to the global public, which we hold in trust for future generations. Apart from our global ecological system, our shared resources include all creations of nature and society, including our genes, our shared knowledge, our airspace and indeed outer space.
>
> In their "race to the bottom" for economic dominance, our governments have neglected their responsibility to protect their citizens' right to their commons, and given free reign instead to private corporations who continue to seize our common wealth by means of enclosure (the ongoing

silent theft of public resources for private financial gain).
. . . As expected, the harshest effects of privatisation and
enclosure are felt in struggling economies, such as parts of
sub-Saharan Africa. In such regions, citizens already living
in poverty are forced to pay exorbitant premiums for priva-
tised essentials such as water, often without seeing significant improvements in supply and provision.

. . . Without a sustainable model for resources management, corporations exploit and consume resources faster
than they can be regenerated or renewed, and levels of waste
and pollution from production exceed the planet's ability to
harmlessly absorb them.

Environmental and social effects of corporate operations
are not accounted for in their balance sheets, they are simply considered "externalities" and consequences of production, thus perverting the true cost of produce which is paid
not by the corporation or the consumer, but initially by
the local people who depend upon the area and ultimately
[by] the global biosphere and the global public. . . . The wave
of enclosure and privatisation can only be brought under
public control by the combined efforts of the global public
through their governments. In order to create a significant
shift in the political and economic ideology, the separation
of governments from the influence of corporations must be
demanded, and the mandates of the undemocratic International Financial Institutions must be progressively disman-
tled and brought under the auspices of the United Nations
and its specialist agencies.

It is crucial, however, that absolute ownership of a given
resource is not simply transferred from "the corporation"
to "the nation" where it may naturally occur. For there to
be a workable, efficient economic system based on sharing
that can redistribute essential resources globally according to
need, it must be understood that all common resources, where
ever they occur on the planet, must be cooperatively owned,
managed and utilised equitably by the global public. . . . Only

through global participation and cooperation can our common assets be reclaimed and their governance shared by society, represented through democratic governments.

In light of this lack of control of governments over the global commons of water and mineral resources, we can ask ourselves, "Who owns and controls the money, our financial commons? Who has the power to decide how we make our exchanges with one another, how we run our economy and make it work?" We can say it is the banks or our government, but shouldn't we say: "It is clear that it also needs to be us"?

We need to wake up and see clearly, both as individuals and collectively, what needs to be done. As I was writing this book and through my conversations with Hazel Henderson, I realized much more deeply how much the resolution of these economic and financial issues is a matter of community. We often seem to be dealing with a world outside of ourselves that we feel we cannot control, dealing with governments or big corporations that seem to be out of our reach. We create this whole situation together and suffer from and buy into a shared illusion around money and a confusion about the place of money in our lives.

Ernie Robson says:

> Perhaps the most important productive outcome from this book, and the web-based interactive financial policy discussion we will enable, is the true answer . . . that we as humans need to change the financial decision-making process itself . . . We each need to be better educated and more involved. We can never again abdicate responsibility for our global financial commons and "money" (and related political power) to anyone who does not put care first!

CHAPTER 16

THE NEW FOUNDATION AND THE SUN

The phrase "global financial commons" speaks of the maturity we need. It is the free and conscious participation of each of us in our world community; it is our planetary citizenship. We are all connected, living on this Earth together, and we cannot escape that fact.

Ellen Brown says in her book *The Web of Debt,*

> Our financial woes are a direct result of a monetary scheme in which money is created by private banks and lent into the economy at interest. To find our way out of the labyrinth, we need to retrace our steps and exit on the road by which we came. The power to create the nation's money and credit needs to be vested in the people themselves.[84]

The pain of isolation, separation, loneliness, and the lack of social, financial, emotional, and spiritual support we can experience in our lives with money need to be healed by establishing a new foundation and support system for our whole economic and financial world. That foundation is based on caring or "caring economics," as Riane Eisler calls it. The mystery here is that we open up the door to our future and walk into this new land by letting caring lead the way in all things. "Care-first" is a phrase we can use, like "Sustainability."

Care-first says: "In the world of money, the wild ride stops and the global casino closes, when we let care do the deciding in all money matters." (By using the term "global casino" we only refer to the misuse of money in trading, not to the stock market itself.) This new land is the world of our global financial commons. All is interconnected. However, we do not lose our individuality. Instead, we are more defined as to who we really are: a unique presence within a world community. The most beautiful flower in nature radiates its uniqueness, yet it is also a complete part of the connected whole.

That connectedness is our home. There we can relax and say, "Money is a part of the global commons, it is a part of the gift, and it is needed by everyone and needs to be available to everyone." Private ownership of money is beautiful, as long as we steward it and do not become too possessive. Stewardship is based on gratitude for what we have received, with the basic understanding that money is never really "mine," nor are any of my assets.

Somehow, we do not need to be afraid of losing our assets, as there maybe isn't anything to lose. It is only when we hold on to things in private ownership with its legal protections and choose not to share that the fear of losing things builds up. The fear of being without money should not really exist, or would not exist if money were made available to all and were created by us all for all. That is where I see the change. It is like the sun warming us and making money available to all.

The global financial commons is a new concept for our hearts and minds in the sense that it describes *a new reality of finance*. When we see money as a part of the global commons, we view it like water and air: something we all need, something that assists us all. We can build our financial kingdom individually and as corporations, and we can imagine ourselves to be ruling the world with "money power." When we drop this idea and serve humanity and the well-being of our planet with our finances, we enter the world of our global financial commons. We can then look at money in a totally different way. We can then see it as a gift to us all for us to share, a gift to bless us all. Let's steward all we own and be grateful for what we have received.

A global financial commons is a space where we look at each other's behavior and actions with money and where those actions can be viewed based on their intention, integrity, and quality. Actions that are harmful and hurt others and the Earth might receive disciplinary action. *A new morality enters our financial world and our conscience, and we will be held accountable for our actions with money.*

This can be the foundation of new health in our financial and economic worlds; a new point of reference for us all; a new common ground in thinking, feeling, and action, where we see money as a servant and not as something that controls our lives and makes us suffer. We allow money to flow differently and, as Barbara Wilder says in *Money Is Love,* "Money is the blood of the planet. Heal the money and we can heal the world."[85] This new flow of money we call a flow of golden water, with money moved by love and care, healing wounds. In 1996, I stated: "Golden Water, healing the wounds of not sharing!"

Money can lift us all into a place where we truly serve one another instead of separating us from one another, from ourselves, and from the Earth. It can unite us to a greater purpose. Money is a test that can bring out the worst and the best in us. It brings out the best when we become more of who we are through money. Money can empower us to live the life we want and to share that life with others. Money is fluidity in the sense that we direct its flow all the time. It is a means of exchange, but it is also more. It can be a lot of things, and everything is moved by our intention.

Our intention can be to support one another, to express gratitude, to bring things together, to stimulate business, to invest, to store and save money in banks and other places, and to create a portal for love—meaning to let money care for the people and the Earth. This intention creates the actual quality of the money itself.

What happens when we create our monetary system with the right intention? In a debt-based monetary system with compound interest, we create a very unhealthy foundation that can be deeply imbued by greed. We can also create a healthy foundation for the issue of currency that is completely constructive. We have different options. We can investigate each of these possibilities and then choose what is appropriate. Hazel and I have been speaking about the possibility of connecting currency to solar energy. As we were speaking, I found myself deeply inspired by the image of the sun, illuminating our life with money. In that process, I received a beautiful inspiration that I will share with you later in this chapter.

Our need for money can create a conflict between our hearts and heads when we feel that needing money is forcing us to do things that we do not believe in and that go against our will, hurt others, and make us sick. Acquiring money, working hard to provide for our families, for ourselves, and maybe for our community makes us feel good when done with joy, without stress, and when it makes us more of who we really are. There are a lot of things stopping us from achieving this state. The following seven things can stop us from being in a constructive flow with money:

1. Doing work we do not love.
2. Feeling we have no choice and need to do things we do not want to do.
3. Seeing money as a negative manifestation and the cause of all evil, as something that only creates harm.
4. Not seeing that money can be good; not seeing that we can direct its use; feeling that it controls us.
5. Seeing the God of Money as an enemy who is trying to hold us down instead of recognizing the resurrection that comes from his death and from his rebirth as the Prince of Peace.
6. Feeling that money works against us from the outside in, meaning that we can be controlled by circumstances instead of being able to create our lives and money ourselves, as we wish.
7. Having a lack of imagination and willingness to share; fear, greed, selfishness, possessiveness, and desire for power; living in the belief that there will never be enough and that we do not deserve an abundant life.

How then can we create our money so it works for us all, and what function do we give it? Our currency was based on gold. It isn't anymore. Perhaps our starting point, a debt-based money system and its compound interest, together with the power and place we have given money in our world, is not the right place to start. We need to decide how we want to live together on this planet and then let money serve that purpose.

I would like the currency we create to be abundant like the fullness of our heart and the Mother's love, like the light of the sun. It needs to allow and encourage our best minds and hearts to solve humanity's problems, not add to them. *With a new monetary system, we rebuild our world.* We can let good business thrive. We can let go of goods and services we do not need and we can make sure that whatever system we create, there is a guarantee and protection in place for the provision of our four basic human rights, so that no one is left out and falls by the wayside.

We can create new currencies and caring financial institutions locally, nationally, and internationally. We have shown in several places in this book that it is already beginning. My belief is that we can start with the money and currencies we already have and redirect their use. We cannot only let private banks run the show. Many have failed humanity by their greed and unnecessary complexity. Their record is clear. Many will make themselves more wealthy and beggar everyone else. A number of the world's private bankers have proven, beyond a doubt, that they do not care enough for the people and the planet first.

We all need to watch out for the same tendencies inside ourselves, and there is no need to point fingers. We are learning together and are faced with the similar choices all the time. It is important to become clear about how we work together within our global financial commons.

The whole process of creating money and releasing it into the system needs to start where we all want it to start. Whatever plan we make needs to truly serve us and apply care-first. We need to work with the receiving, sharing, and stewarding of the gifts bestowed upon all of us and on our country. We also need input into how money flows on a state and local level. We will need to review the fractional reserve system[86] and the interest-bearing procedures. Collectively, we need to use the ingenuity it took to create our present money system, banking, insurance, commodity trading, and stock markets, not to mention private venture capital, and apply this problem-solving ability to finding solutions to remedy our money system.

It is critical to have our currency backed by something real like energy or some other measure of economic development, not just be created out of thin air. I don't think currency should be placed against a finite resource. Money needs to be abundant, not finite. Hazel Henderson has started speaking about using solar energy to create a universal unit of value for the currency we need. For more information about the relationship between currency and energy, read note.[87]

I find the idea of connecting finance to the sun very inspiring. I know that serious attempts are being made to see how a currency can be created based on energy, on electricity, and on kilowatt hours. For the moment, I just want us to approach this with an open mind and in a state of wonder about the possibilities and positive aspects of relating a currency to the sun through solar energy. I want to share with you a visual inspiration I received exactly as it came to me about the creation and function of money inspired by energy of the sun.

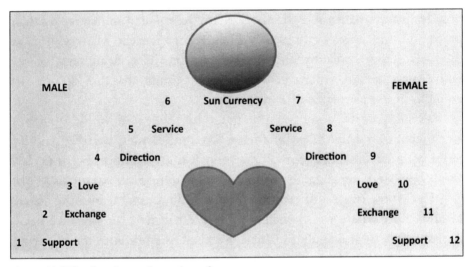

Figure 16.1 The function and creation of money.

It was a beautiful experience, showing me six functions of money held in a perfect balance of male and female energy (often creative processes happen through a balance of these two):

- To support us all
- To be a great medium of exchange
- To be a tool for us to express our love
- To direct us
- To serve all it meets
- To be abundant like the sun

Ernie Robson says: "Energy, like anything else, is subject to change. Currently, like gold, energy is scarce. But in the future, with innovation and attention, it can be as abundant as solar energy. This is what happened with the vast discoveries of gold and silver in the US in the 1800s. There was, at first, tremendous economic expansion; then, as we returned to just gold as a standard for our money system worldwide, the supply of gold (and hence money) limited our growth and was a major cause of the Great Depression of the 1930s. When a new and cheap and plentiful and environmentally safe energy is created by our ingenuity, then, once again, we will be discussing what to do next with our money systems."

CHAPTER 17

THE POWER OF CARE

We are in a paradigm shift. To shift from a debt-based monetary system (with compound interest), so much influenced by greed and selfishness, to a possible monetary system based on energy (maybe from the sun), based on our sharing heart and abundance, is a huge shift. There is nothing to say that we cannot do this.

In order to help us make this shift, I want to say more about the power of care and look more deeply at the concepts of care-first and money-first. I really have found that care is like a threshold to money, meaning that our money world needs to be touched by care and then money can be a means to assist our economic world to be transformed into a very constructive world.

We can form all the concepts we want about how to run a new economy and create the financial world we want, but without the application of care for ourselves, for each other, and for our planet, we have no foundation. Care is like a beacon of light. Wherever we apply it, things heal.

This care also applies itself to ourselves. When we apply care-first to ourselves, we acknowledge and support ourselves and make sure that we are well. This is something we can very easily forget. I sometimes call it angel's disease: many people with open hearts are like angels. They find it so easy to care for others, but much more difficult to care for themselves, as if it is a blind spot.

Because we are the beginning of our actions, we need that care to be applied to ourselves. What is the quality of our actions going to be if we are not well? And of course how we treat ourselves is often how we will treat others.

How do we listen to that care for ourselves, for each other, and for our planet? Care is in a certain sense an unfamiliar energy in our culture. It can look like it is very familiar to us all because to care for each other seems to be such a natural expression in ourselves. We so easily care for our children, family, and friends. But there are so many places and areas in our culture where care is not applied, and there it looks like we do not know what it is to care or what care is.

I said in the beginning of the book that the relationship between money and care is very important. In our dealings with money we are constantly challenged in that care. There is a field of constant tension between our money-first and care-first attitudes inside each of us, which creates either a money-first or care-first world and economy.

We apply care-first when we put care first
and let money serve that care.
We apply money-first when we put money first
at the expense of what we care about.
I see money-first and care-first as the two aspects of our test with money.

In a care-first world,
we use money in service of our caring, our values, and our passion.
We use it in service of the well-being
of ourselves, each other and the Earth.
care-first creates a love-based economy.

In a money-first world
we use money at the expense of our caring, our values, and our passion.
We use it at the expense of the well-being
of ourselves, of each other, and of the Earth.
Money-first creates a fear-based economy.

As we enter the money-first aspect of our life and culture, we meet an illusion.
We look for money without looking for caring, life, and spirit and
hope to find something but enter emptiness and find nothing.
This can lead to anger and frustration and can open the careless
and destructive side of our nature.

As we enter the care-first aspect of our life and culture, we meet truth.
When we aim for caring, life, and spirit and use money to serve that aim,
we enter fullness and find everything.
This leads to satisfaction and happiness and opens the caring
and constructive side of our nature.

When we look at care-first and money-first inside ourselves
we can see that when we live in money-first,
we are tense, alone, in separation, fearful, and depressed.
When we live in care-first,
we are strong, vibrant, happy, and, most of all, in harmony with ourselves.

Care-first stabilizes the world, because it stabilizes our psyche.
Care-first sustains the world because it sustains us.
Money-first destabilizes the world and is not sustainable.
Can you see what will happen to our world when we move from
a money-first to a care-first attitude?

THE POWER OF CARE

Let's look at money-first and care-first
in the light of manifesting what we need.
Both are intimately connected to how we survive and make a living.
Because money is the provider of so many things, we need it.
Our common sense sees that and the main path we take is to work for that money.

In that sense very often we put money first, because we need it so badly.
Everyone knows that this doesn't necessarily lead to happiness, especially if
we are not happy in the work that we do.
In care-first, we manifest all that we need through care.
Care is a very powerful reality.

Most people in this world live by the premise that in order to eat, sleep, and drink
we need money and do not question this premise.
This often results in an unconscious anger and frustration
and also a feeling of being victimized by a world we are a part of and born into,
but cannot change.

*"This is what the world is like
and we'd better make the best of what we have,"
not realizing that there are other options
and that we have the power to create
the world we want.*

*I came to realize that this is the premise of the world of money-first
and that there is another option,
which is that we can begin to love and experience the power of that love.
This led me to the concept of care-first;
care, of course, being love in action.*

*I understood the following thing:
Money-first holds the premise that we need the money first
and then we can have what we want.
Money is the provider here and
we need to put our focus on the money.*

*The premise of care-first is
that care holds the power
and is the provider
and we need to focus on the care
for our well-being, survival, and money.*

*The care creates the money
The money serves the care.
The source provides.
We can create all our finances
by the action of love alone.*

*This is a simple shift in our heart, soul, and mind.
The care becomes the opener of the way and guides us along a very different path.
We are guided by the care for ourselves, each other, and our planet Earth,
which really is being guided by love.
Love and care as the movers of our economic behavior.*

When I wrote the sentence, "We create all our finances by the action of love alone" in 2002, I felt it was true, but also felt it was quite stretch. Now, in 2011, I feel as a result of the experiences of my life that this is absolutely true, even in the midst of the difficult times we are having.

We all deal with the world around us and the circumstances we have created; but as I shared in "Our Personal Story," I have had so many experiences in my life where I felt that Life, the spiritual world, or whatever words you want to give it, cares for us. It provides us with very powerful tools for creating our own life. Now I can truly state:

We can also experience the source of our sustenance
inside ourselves as our connection to the Divine,
which regulates our life out of a true caring for our soul's path.
Through this alignment, we know that all material things that we are in need of
will come our way, if circumstance allows.

CHAPTER 18

OUR COMPANIES AND OUR WORK

We created our Scottish charitable company, World Finance Initiative, in 1996, while we were running a small retreat center high up in Scotland, 70 miles north of Inverness. In 2006, we created our trading subsidiary (the for-profit branch of the charity) called CareFirstWorld Ltd. Sandra and I and our dear friend Gabriella Kapfer from Germany, now living the UK, have been running this company according to principles we all believe in. Our mission statement says:

> Everything we steward in the Company we see as part of the Earth's gift to us all and we hold it as such and see ourselves as caretakers of these assets. We use them for the purpose of sharing: to assist us in sharing our work and talents and to share the assets themselves where appropriate. We see the finance in the Company as money for everyone and as money to care with. We decide as to how that caring with money applies itself: towards our own needs, the path of the Company, and all it serves.

> We experience the Earth and all that it provides as a gift to us all, for us to receive, share, and steward together. We feel that everyone has an equal right to food, shelter, education, and health care and all that life provides. We see that as a

universal human right, and our focus is to make sure that each one of us is alright. We also see money as a human right. Let money be there for all, let it go round, let it care.

Gabriella, Sandra, and I are directors of CareFirstWorld Ltd. and have worked with the principle of income-sharing from the beginning. All our income goes into the company and we receive a weekly basic income to cover our living expenses. Two percent of all our income goes to World Finance Initiative and supports other charities. We also support our Community Care Bank.

We keep track of what we give and receive from the company and keep this in balance. The beauty of all this is that we feel we are not alone in our survival and can support each other where needed at any moment in time. We also make decisions together in relation to what we do with our "extras" and that is how the idea for the Community Care Bank emerged.

We have successfully managed this while living in different locations such as Scotland, Holland, and England. All our income flows into the company. It not so much different from just dealing with our own private circulation of money, because we do draw out most of what we put in. It is the shared space we created among ourselves that is such a relief from just doing it on our own and makes it all very different.

We have worked with three parts of the Initiative for a long time: our School of Care, our Care Fund, and our Care-First Community. All three are ways to assist us all through the transition, moving from the old to the new, as described below in this short list of problems and how we assist one another in resolving them.

THE WORK OF THE WORLD FINANCE INITIATIVE

OUR PROBLEMS

PROBLEMS WITH MONEY

- Money tensions and worries
- Feeling victimized by the money system
- Seeing money as a necessary evil.

PROBLEMS WITH WORK

- Doing work we do not love
- Not enough time for ourselves and family
- Physical complaints due to work

PROBLEMS WITH SURVIVAL

- Standing too much on our own
- Not receiving enough help and support
- Too much responsibility on our shoulders

OUR WORK WITH THE WORLD FINANCE INITIATIVE

THE CARE FUND
Creating a constructive flow of money

THE SCHOOL OF CARE
Finding our true talents

CARE-FIRST COMMUNITY
Stimulating community support and care

OUR SOLUTIONS

SOLUTIONS ABOUT MONEY

- Making financial transactions constructive
- Letting money serve our care
- Giving our economy a love-based foundation

SOLUTIONS ABOUT WORK

- To do the work we love
- To have a place in our community
- To serve the well-being of people and the Earth

SOLUTIONS ABOUT SURVIVAL

- To help each other
- To share tasks, skills, and goals
- To apply care to everything

The Care Fund *(our Community Care Bank)* is a fund we've created in World Finance Initiative and in our Dutch charity, Zorg Eerst Projecten (Care First Projects). We use money to help each other, to care for one another, to share, to give, and to receive. In 2010 we made a small beginning with a new idea and planted its first seed, but we are still in the experimental stage: *We give, we loan, and invest . . . The money in the Fund comes from all who join the Gifting Circle, where we let the money go round. It can reach situations that might not have found a way to receive help otherwise.*

The idea is that anyone can join and become a Friend of the Gifting Circle by making their contribution into the circle. As a Friend, anyone can make a request to help someone else in need.

This request gets processed by us and then we decide whether the course of action proposed is truly empowering to the receiver. We then allocate the money to the receiver. Besides assisting each other locally and nationally (in the United Kingdom and the Netherlands at the moment) we aim to share and care internationally and we will see how to develop this.

We want money to go around in a caring and sharing manner and let a small percentage flow into four particular areas we wish to serve: homelessness, children, women, and our Earth.

Our School of Care is run by Sandra and myself, together with Gabriella Kapfer. We all work internationally. All three of us offer our educational and therapeutic work in the School of Care. You can find out more about Gabriella's activities at *www.peace-trails.com* and Sandra's and my activities at *www.CareFirstWorld.com*. In the School of Care, we assist each other to find our gift(s), our deepest and truest expression in life, and we work together to create a new economic foundation for bringing that unique contribution to our world community. The transition from a job or manner of surviving with which we are not fully happy to a place where we feel truly fulfilled is often not easy. To manage this transition financially can be a challenge. This transition often requires deep soul-searching to find out what we really want to do in life. We use self-development tools to receive assistance with this particular process.

Our Care-First Community is a worldwide network of friends and colleagues we have worked with over a period of twenty-six years, who work with aspects of our vision in their own way; we constantly grow together. We have stimulated a lot of community activity in Holland, England, Scotland, and the United States over the years. Our workshop "Meeting the Mystery of Money" activated this in different places, especially in Virginia and in the South of England.

In the logo of the World Finance Initiative, you see a blue pot, from which a Greek Goddess pours golden water. We created a blue pot out of clay, which we use for receiving contributions; we have very successfully worked with it since 1990. The principle is that we work without a fixed charge, but offer people a sliding scale or a suggested fee when they need that. People are asked to make a love-based contribution to support our work. This blue pot has created a lot of magic everywhere, and love and sharing among people. It seems to be a very natural way to exchange money; it calls forth the spontaneity and nature of the heart.

Using a fixed charge, which is the foundation of all business, is a very necessary and functional answer. We use this as well as our blue pot. We can apply our hearts and minds to different ways of making a transaction and be creative with it. What matters is whether it works and makes us happy. I always say that gifting, which is what we do with the blue pot, is a very pure energy in us all. There are lot of people in our network who are using and have used that blue pot. The Goddess of Abundance in the workshop, holding the blue pot in the air, says: "This is my heart. This is how we share. Let's heal our planet."

The intention behind starting to use it was that Sandra and I, in 1990, decided that in our work we just wanted to share our gift and make it possible for anyone to receive the help they needed. We made the work that needed doing come first and allowed the money serve that. We did not want someone to sit in a session, deep in their process, needing to decide whether they could afford another hour of work or not. We wanted people to just have space for whatever was going on. Many people have felt very grateful for this and love the blue pot. They have really cared for us, they pay us what they can and sometimes more, and often share a lot with us. It has definitely created a whole new world among us. What is also interesting is that when we do this in a workshop, something naturally balances itself out between those who can afford more and those who can afford less. The total amount we receive very often feels just right and expresses that natural balance between those with different income levels.

All three of us use the blue pot very often. We constantly look at what the most constructive and caring way is for us to exchange finance and care for one another. We have lived, since 1990, in different community settings and have applied all this sharing and caring very successfully. We have built up a lot of trust among many people over the years, and we know we can rely upon each other when we need something or are in trouble. All the things I speak of and propose we have lived and experienced. I just would like to apply them on a much larger scale.

We have carried and lived with our vision and shared it everywhere, but we realized that the application of it was challenging for many. At some point, I realized that when it comes to money, we so quickly move into our heads and that I needed to assist people to work with themselves in a much deeper way. This intention created our workshop "Meeting the Mystery of Money" in 2003.

MEETING THE MYSTERY OF MONEY

Below I share with you the leaflet we use for this workshop:

> In this intensive, we explore our relationship to money on a deeply experiential and cellular level, explore and transform old patterns and core beliefs, and are assisted in moving from fear to trust. It is a threshold-crossing experience in which money is the portal to a higher level of community, to a higher world of light. The process is alchemical and is held in sacred ceremony throughout. It portrays the archetypal story behind our relationship with money, its purpose, challenge, and outcome and sets a new tone for the future of economics.
>
> We are looking at a constructive use of money and creating a sharing world. We learn to apply care-first, using money in service of our values, for the well-being of all and for our planet, and not at their expense. With the loving support of five facilitators who each represent an archetype:

The God of Money, the Goddess of Abundance, the Community Keeper, the Condor, and the Eagle, and the use of sacred ceremony, music, and masks, we start a very personal and communal journey through the land of money (see Chapter 5 for more details).

Here is what some of our workshop participants have said about their experiences:

I have taken many workshops, but this workshop "Meeting the Mystery of Money" is within my heart the single most powerful experiential workshop I have taken to date. This 2-day intensive works on a cellular level and has completely regenerated my experience with money. My personal experience with money in the past was not that I held no value toward it. I could see that I was, in fact, not holding enough "value" for myself and my work in the world, where money was concerned. Immediately following the workshop I began to incorporate the "blue pot" into my work. I have doubled my earnings in very little time. In short, my world has been transformed.—*D. C., Orillia, Ontario, Canada*

★ ★ ★

I rarely sign up for workshops, but I felt these very Earth-connected chosen guides are fulfilling the seed of building a new paradigm community. This workshop brought my fears around money to a higher clarity for release in such a profound way. It then revealed how we can build a trusting community providing much greater awareness and support for each other.—*V. A. W., Charlottesville, Virginia*

★ ★ ★

The workshop (intensive) is a unique, experiential, and interactive opportunity to discover, explore, and transform old patterns/core beliefs that block one from fully experiencing financial abundance in their life. Through this deeper unfolding of personal insights and revelations, one is able to discover what is really going on beneath the surface in creating their financial reality and how those beliefs or attitudes relate to personal creativity and community. Louis and Sandra embody the enthusiasm and inspiration necessary in co-creating a love-based approach for both community and finance and provide a safe, nurturing space for participants. This workshop is truly life-changing.—*P. S., Staunton, Virginia*

CHAPTER 19

HOPE FOR THE FUTURE: WHAT WE CAN DO

I dedicate this chapter to Hazel Henderson. Today (November 23, 2010) we completed our last writing session together, on the evening of my 18th day in Florida. In dedicating it to her, I quote Fritjof Capra who, in 1988, wrote the foreword to her book, *The Politics of the Solar Age: Alternatives to Economics*.

> As we are approaching the end of the 1980s it is becoming increasingly apparent that the major problems of our time cannot be understood in isolation. Most economic concepts and models are no longer adequate to understand economic phenomena in a fundamentally interdependent world. Hazel Henderson, futurist, environmentalist, and economic iconoclast, has been driving home this point for over a decade with an intensity, brilliance, and originality still unmatched today. She has challenged the world's foremost economists, politicians and corporate leaders with her well-founded critique of their fundamental concepts and values. Because of her talent for presenting her radical ideas in a disarming, nonthreatening manner, her voice is heard and respected in government and corporate circles; she has held an impressive number of advisory positions and has cofounded and directed numerous organisations, in which her new ways of thinking are elaborated and applied.

I completely agree with this description of her. I share it not just to honor her, but also to use the example of her life to stimulate us all to make the changes we need and to persevere. It is clear at this moment in time that people are very upset about how banks have dealt with the mortgage-based securities and CDOs and how all that speculation and lack of care has severely disrupted our economic and financial well-being. It is a very difficult moment in time all over the planet, economically and financially. Many of us are really looking for answers.

Hazel has been standing by what she has felt and voiced it throughout her life. I have been doing the same, but I can be quite insecure at times, and I am sure that many of us can doubt whether we see things correctly, question the love we feel, and even feel hesitant to fully express ourselves. But we can and need to come forward with our deepest values, no matter what the world around us looks like, and speak up and keep viewing the world from our childlike wonderment and clarity.

My question is: What can we do together and how can we do it? There are so many people working for positive change. When I think of the thirty million people backing the petition to propose changes in how we measure GDP, as discussed in Chapter 3, which Hazel Henderson has been promoting for eons, it shows what we can do. Riane Eisler is doing so much to promote a Caring Economics. You can read more about that on her website, *www.partnershipway.org*. There are many people working tirelessly to create positive change. I have offered many examples of these positive efforts, which we do not often hear about. I want to share two more great examples that show what we can do, when we persist and follow our heart.

THE MAN WHO PLANTED TREES[88]

The Man Who Planted Trees is a book about an inspiring person. Here is a book review about it by Bobby Matherne:[89]

> This delightful book was written by "The Man Who Planted Words," Jean Giono. On the barren slopes of Provence, the old Roman province in France with the California weather, the narrator encounters a shepherd [Elezeard Bouffier] and

stays overnight with him. The next day he notices that the water-soaked acorns the shepherd had so carefully culled the previous evening are intended as seeds for oak trees. Invited by the shepherd, he accompanies him on his rounds for the day, which consist of him punching a hole in the ground with his iron staff, placing an acorn in the hole, and covering it with dirt. As they plant trees, the old man (in his fifties in the 1910 setting of the start of the story), explains that he has planted over 100,000 acorns so far, and expects 10,000 oaks to grow from them.

He shows Giono his fenced-in plot of birch seedlings that he has planned for the river bottoms where ancient streams once ran. The narrator returns after the war of 1917 and finds a great young forest covering the previously barren hills and the shepherd, untouched by war, still planting trees. After the war in 1939, the narrator returns to find brooks flowing over dried out traces, new homes, and hearty young people in a bustling village where only three hermits had lived before. . . .

Long referred to as "the most dangerous animal," it is time to remember that man is "the most caring animal." The shepherd lived in a future that included trees, forests, and brooks and, working his way backwards to the present, began planting the seeds to create the future he envisioned. "Uncaring" is a feature of man's nature whereas "caring" is a byproduct of his highest human capability, the ability to "see things that never were and ask why not," in Bobby Kennedy's words.

RYAN'S WELL: HOW A 6-YEAR-OLD STARTED CHANGING THE WORLD

Below is a reprint of an article by Arielle Ford. It appeared on the *Giam Life* website, *life.gaiam.com*:[90]

Ryan Hreljac was in kindergarten when he learned that children in a Ugandan village had to walk many kilometers every day just for fresh drinking water. Dismayed, he set out to do enough chores to raise the $70 he figured it would take to drill a well for the village. It turned out the well would cost more like $2,000 to drill—but Ryan was undaunted, and he raised close to $3,000 that year as his story made headlines.

Pictured to the left [in the original article] at age 9 with his Ugandan penpal, Jimmy, Ryan was finally able to travel to the Ugandan village where his penpal lived and where one of his wells was being built. A film crew began documenting how Ryan's wells improve living conditions for entire villages and free up precious time for youngsters to go to school. The short film *Ryan's Well* is available on DVD from Earth Cinema Circle. Ryan is now [2008] a 6' 6" 16-year-old, and The Ryan's Well Foundation has raised more than $1 million and built 319 wells that provide clean drinking water to 485,433 people in 14 countries.

Actor Matt Damon and his nonprofit organization, Africa H2O, recently committed $200,000 to The Ryan's Well Foundation [*www.ryanswell.ca*] through a matching funds initiative. "It will help bring clean water to thousands more people and help us achieve what many thought was impossible," says Ryan of Damon's support. Any kid can follow his lead, says Ryan. "Kids can begin with anything from helping out around the house to starting their own project," he adds. They're real words of wisdom, coming from this boy who considered himself, at age 6, just as responsible as anyone else for solving a problem affecting people a world away.

What these stories tell me is that when we truly care and want to do something about a particular situation, we can. When we stay focused and work steadily and tirelessly, like Ryan and the shepherd Elezeard, we should be able to let the golden water flow in our financial world. I have faith in all of us.

In my 30-year-experience of working with people's deepest issues, I know that regardless of whatever darkness we experience, each one of us carries a light in our hearts and has the potential to step forward and become the best we can be.

I know that, somehow, we can make our voices heard; each of us, with our unique gifts and talents, can come forward and join forces with all who are working towards the same goal. Let's help each other to do so. That is why we open up the space with this book for anyone to come forward with inspirations and ideas about what we can do together to help create an economic and financial world we love.

A PLAN OF ACTION

Let's look at a plan of action. I would like us to explore together how to revise our monetary system; how we want to create our money, and who would do it, and how it would be made available and distributed. We do this for us to come to clarity around how we can fulfill of our four basic needs for home, food, education, and health care, to see how we can create the space for each of us to make our unique contribution in the work we do, and to see how we take care of all remaining practical tasks and chores.

It is clear that we need to deal with this on a worldwide level, a country level, on local and individual levels. Many people have the possibility and freedom to take any initiative locally; any province or state can make decisions about these things, as can countries as a whole. Because of the interconnectedness and interdependence of today's world, it is clear that we also need to make decisions on a worldwide scale.

Looking at what is going on in the United States at the moment and how the instability of the whole system, worldwide, affects many countries, we need to wake up and make that needed shift. Otherwise, we can expect collapse at any time. Fundamental reform can look like a daunting task; many people might say: "How do we deal with those who have more control over this situation than others, whether they are in government, banks, or businesses?" My response to this is that all of us, whatever our position of power, need something better than what we have. Each of us needs to create clarity in our minds and hearts about what is needed for our children and for generations to come. I have total faith in our capacity to do so. This book is intended to provide inspiration, hope, and ideas about how we can do that.

One of the most difficult and persistent problems we have is the gap between the rich and the poor. In July 2011, I received updated information from Rajesh Makwana, executive director of Share The World's Resources (*www.stwr.org*), in a letter he wrote to me on this subject:

The income gap between the richest and poorest people has generally increased both between and within countries for the past 30 years. At the same time, the least well off in society—the world's 'bottom billion'—are becoming collectively poorer as their share of global income has reduced significantly over the same period. If we include household wealth in this assessment the picture is even more unequal, with over half of all global wealth owned by the richest 2 percent, 40 percent of wealth owned by the top 1 percent, and 85 percent owned by the top 10 percent. In comparison, a mere 1 percent of total global wealth is shared by half of the world's population.

The most striking reflection of global inequality is the stark contrast between the plight of the world's poorest people and the growing fortunes of the ultra rich. According to the World Health Organisation's most recent statistics, at least 41,000 people die each day from a small group of preventable conditions that include diarrhea, measles and nutritional deficiencies. This amounts to over 15 million preventable deaths each year that occur almost exclusively in the developing world as a direct consequence of poverty. The prevalence of such extreme deprivation is entirely unnecessary given the amount of wealth and resources that exist. The latest World Wealth Report by Merrill Lynch and Capgemini revealed that, despite the global financial crisis of 2008, the wealth of High Net Worth Individuals (HNWI) has reached record levels. Between 2009 and 2010, the combined fortunes of this exclusive group of less than 11 million individuals increased by 10 percent to a high of $42.7 trillion. The huge amount of income and wealth available in the world today shows how easily we could overcome poverty if resources were more equally distributed.

I am sure many of us have heard similar figures over and over again. I don't know of an approach yet that fundamentally closes that gap and creates true equality among us all. Many people share, and we often share a lot, especially in times of crisis, and that always tells me that we should be able do it. I always feel that sharing is natural to us all. What are we are going to need to do to resolve the ridiculous situation in which half of the world's population (the poorest) owns one percent of things and ten percent of our world's population (the richest) own eighty-five percent?

I feel it is time, and we are at a crucial starting point, to place sharing at the heart of our financial world, our banking systems and of our financial policies for the recognition of our financial commons.

CHAPTER 20

INVESTING MONEY WHERE OUR VALUES ARE

Let's look at investing in the future, putting our money where our values are, exemplifying fairness and creating a green economy. Let's explore Socially Responsible Investing, Green America, Ethical Markets, and Fair Trade.

SOCIALLY RESPONSIBLE INVESTING

Socially Responsible Investing (SRI) is a broad-based approach to investing that now encompasses an estimated $3.07 trillion out of $25.2 trillion in the U.S. investment marketplace as of 2011.[91] SRI recognizes that corporate responsibility and societal concerns are valid parts of investment decisions. SRI considers both the investor's financial needs and an investment's impact on society.

SRI investors encourage corporations to improve their practices on environmental, social, and governance issues. You may also hear SRI-like approaches to investing referred to as mission investing, responsible investing, double or triple bottom-line investing, ethical investing, sustainable investing, or green investing.

As a result of its investing strategies, SRI also works to enhance the bottom lines of the companies in question and, in so doing, delivers more long-term wealth to shareholders. In addition, SRI investors seek to build wealth in underserved communities worldwide. With SRI, investors can put their money to work to build a more sustainable world while earning competitive returns both today and over time. Socially responsible investors include individuals and also institutions, such as corporations, universities, hospitals, foundations, insurance companies, public and private pension funds, nonprofit organizations, and religious institutions. Institutional investors represent the largest and fastest growing segment of the SRI world.

Hazel Henderson writes about the future of Socially Responsible Investing in her 2006 book *Ethical Markets: Growing the Green Economy*:

> Three pillars of SRI are: 1) social, environmental auditing, or ethical screening; 2) community investing; and 3) shareholder activism. The fourth pillar is socially responsible venture capital, which is vital in seeding new companies needed in the shift to global sustainability.
>
> SRI is active in USA, Canada, Europe, Australia, New Zealand, Japan, China, and Brazil.
>
> On April 27, 2006, representatives of more than 20 pension funds from sixteen countries managing over $2 trillion of assets made the historic announcement at the New York Stock Exchange of their launch of [the United Nations backed] Principles for Responsible Investment. In a matter of weeks, new signatories swelled the total over to $5 trillion. Denise Nappier, treasurer of the State of Connecticut, a long-time leader in SRI, noted "We are proud to endorse the principles, which recognize that social and environmental issues can be material to the financial outlook of a company and therefore to the value of the shares in that company."(more at *www.unpri.org, and www.unepfi.org*). In this book [*Ethical Markets: Growing the Green Economy*] and its Companion TV series, *Ethical Markets* (*www.ethical-markets.tv*), we covered many companies and CEOs creating higher standards and benchmarks for good corporate citizenship in the twenty-first century. The future of this movement for more ethical markets globally promises to be bright.

GREEN AMERICA

Green America, previously known as Co-op America until January 1, 2009, was established in 1982. It is a not-for-profit membership organization. Its mission statement (on *www.greenamerica.org*) says:

> Our mission is to harness economic power—the strength of consumers, investors, businesses, and the marketplace—to create a socially just and environmentally sustainable society. We work for a world where all people have enough, where all communities are healthy and safe, and where the bounty of the Earth is preserved for all the generations to come.[92]

I am introducing you to Hazel Henderson's company Ethical Markets, her *Ethical Markets TV* site (*www.ethicalmarkets.tv*), and the Green Transition Scoreboard (*www.greentransitionscoreboard.com*), which tracks all investment of the private financial system worldwide in the green economy. The following quotes are from their mission statements.

> Ethical Markets' mission is to foster the evolution of capitalism beyond current models based on materialism, maximizing self-interest and profit, competition and fear of scarcity. As we move further into the Information Age, we learn that information and knowledge are not scarce, and our economic models can move toward sharing, cooperating, and a new abundance. We believe capitalism, combined with humanity's growing knowledge of the interdependence of all life on Planet Earth, can evolve to serve today's new needs and our common future—beyond maximizing profits for shareholders and management, to benefiting all stakeholders. We deliver this message to our global market by featuring stories of success.
>
> Ethical Markets showcases the organizations, trade associations, shareholder activities, the mutual funds and pension funds asset managers, financial planners, venture capital groups, innovative technologies and companies, as well as

this vision of maturing, socially-responsible, ethical capitalism fitting humanity's aspirations for a more peaceful, just
and ecologically sustainable world.

Ethical Markets' TV series seeks to foster public understanding of all these issues . . . and awareness of the
new players and the choices they offer to consumers, employees, investors, asset managers, financial planners, and
citizens to align their own lives, work, investment decisions, and daily activities with their own highest goals. By
showcasing all these groups and individuals spearheading
the new ethical markets, we seek to grow this emerging,
job-creating sector and expand its market share—globally
and locally.

Figure 20.1 The Green Transition Scoreboard,
showing investment in green companies.

The following information is from the Green Transition Scoreboard
website (*www.greentransitionscoreboard.com*):

THE GREEN TRANSITION SCOREBOARD® (GTS) is a time-based global tracking of the private financial system for all sectors involved with green markets, producing a transparent line of sight toward the ethical progress of wealth building as defined by the triple bottom line of planet, people, and profits. **The GTS logo represents a visual symbol for inevitable human progress** whose barometer rises, away from the symbols of the out-dated Fossil Fuel Era, as green investments increase over the next ten years and we enter the next economy—the age of light.

The GTS was created and realized by Hazel Henderson and Ethical Markets Media. It is updated and maintained by Ethical Markets Media, LLC. Financial data and organizations included in the GTS are screened by the strictest of rigorous social, environmental, and ethical auditing standards.

The GREEN TRANSITION SCOREBOARD, tracking private sector investments since 2007 in green companies and technologies globally, now totals more than $2 trillion. Data and organizations included in the GTS are screened by the strictest of rigorous social, environmental, and ethical auditing, The Green Transition Scoreboard® represents time-based, global research of non-government investments and commitments for green markets in Renewable Energy, Efficiency and Green Construction, Cleantech, Smart Grid and Corporate R&D. The February 2011 update of the GTS totals $2,005,048,785,088 from 2007 to the end of 2010, significant because many studies indicate that investing $1 trillion annually until 2020 will accelerate the Green Transition worldwide. This updated 2011 finding puts global investors and countries on track to reach the $10 trillion in investments goal by 2020, setting the path for governments and institutional investors to follow.

This is great hope for the future! Let's go for it!

FAIR TRADE
Wikipedia describes Fair Trade as follows:

> Fair Trade is an organized social movement and market-
> based approach that aims to help producers in developing
> countries make better trading conditions and promote sus-
> tainability. The movement advocates the payment of a higher
> price to producers as well as [promoting higher] social and
> environmental standards. In particular, it focuses on exports
> from developing countries to developed countries, most
> notably handicrafts, coffee, cocoa, sugar, tea, bananas, honey,
> cotton, wine, fresh fruit, chocolate, flowers and gold.[93]
>
> In 2008, products certified with FLO's International
> Fairtrade Certification amounted to approximately US$4.08
> billion worldwide, a 22% year-to-year increase. While this
> represents a tiny fraction of world trade in physical mer-
> chandise, some fair trade products account for 20-50% of all
> sales in their product categories in individual countries. In
> June 2008, Fairtrade Labeling Organizations International
> estimated that over 7.5 million producers and their families
> were benefiting from fair trade funded infrastructure, tech-
> nical assistance and community development projects.[94]

Fairtrade UK is an independent nonprofit organization that licenses
the use of the FAIRTRADE mark on products in the UK in accordance
with internationally agreed Fairtrade Standards. It was established in 1992.
According to the Mission Statement of Fairtrade UK (*www.fairtrade.org.uk*):

> Our vision is of a world in which justice and sustainable
> development are at the heart of trade structures and prac-
> tices so that everyone, through their work, can maintain a
> decent and dignified livelihood and develop their full po-
> tential. To achieve this vision, Fairtrade seeks to transform
> trading structures and practices in favour of the poor and
> disadvantaged. By facilitating trading partnerships based on
> equity and transparency, Fairtrade contributes to sustain-

able development for marginalised producers, workers and their communities. Through demonstration of alternatives to conventional trade and other forms of advocacy, the Fairtrade movement empowers citizens to campaign for an international trade system based on justice and fairness.

GUAYAKÍ YERBA MATE

Chris Mann is one of the five founders of Guayakí Yerba Mate (*www.guayaki.com*). His company was founded in 1996. He works with yerba mate farmers in the the South American Atlantic rainforests. On his website he commented:

> Fair Trade is one of the most important global movements happening right now. We now live in a very economic world where we measure things in dollars and cents. People who have gotten pushed to the bottom of that system are the small producers that really hold the wisdom, do the work, and provide food for us. We're very out of touch with all this because it is so far away. The reality is that the purchase decisions we make in the USA have a huge impact on what is happening in the South American rainforest, in Africa, in Asia, all around the world.

Guayakí's mission is to steward and restore 200,000 acres of South American rainforest and create 1000 living wage jobs by 2020. In 2009, Guayakí became the first Fair Trade Certified yerba mate company in the world. [95]

THE JERUSALEM CANDLE

I read a wonderful, touching story in Hazel Henderson's book *Ethical Markets* about Amber Chand, co-creator of the The Jerusalem Candle. Amber Chand says:

> Fair Trade, just look at those words: fair, respectful, open, generous; and trade. Trade is the sacred art of exchange, the

most ancient practice that happened since Asia's Silk Road. It is truly the way human beings function—we trade with each other, we barter with each other. Fair Trade is knowing that we need to treat people with great respect.[96]

In 2004, Amber Chand, founder of the Women's Peace Collection, went to the Middle East with a small group of American businesswomen. After exploring the area, she initiated the creation of the Jerusalem Candle of Hope, a joint venture between Israeli and Palestinian women. It was birthed from a potent vision to bring together women on either side of a conflict through a process of respectful enterprise. Here is the story from her website, *womenspeacecollection.com*:

> Jerusalem is considered the "City of Peace" and The Luminary of Hope a symbol of peace that seeks to transcend borders of conflict. Created by Palestinian and Israeli women, the luminary candle is made of natural beeswax and embedded with olive leaves and everlasting flowers gathered in fields in Nazareth. It comes with an embroidered bag, sewn by Palestinian women in Bethlehem that contains a simple, replaceable tea light. When lit, the candle offers a beautiful glow reflecting an enduring vision for peace.
>
> Our journey led us to the hillsides of Nazareth in Israel, where we discovered a well-known family owned candle making facility that employs newly arrived Russian Jewish immigrant women living in the outlying neighbourhoods. We were told that without consistent orders for candles, many of these women would remain unemployed. When we met with the women and asked how they felt about this collaborative peace building project, they responded, without hesitation: "We do not mind because orders for the candles means food on our table, a roof over our head, and clothes for our children." They went on to speak of the Jerusalem Candle of Hope as a "practical way to support cooperation between people" and an important means to earn a dignified livelihood.

On the other side of the checkpoint, in the West Bank, we came to the home of a Palestinian master embroiderer living in the heart of Bethlehem. From stacks of embroidered designs that she kept in thick photo albums in her bedroom, we designed a small, exquisitely embroidered fabric bag to hold a tea light that would illuminate the candle. We were told that the sale of just 10 of these small, embroidered bags would support a family of four for one day. And that, because of these initial orders, more than 15 embroiderers would be able to support their families in the community. One had already made enough money to buy a wheelchair; another was able to serve chicken—a delicacy—to her family; and another was able to pay for transportation to go to university.

Since the craftswomen could not physically meet each other at this time, we sought the support of The Parents Circle: A Families Forum, who helped us bring together all of these complex elements. This wonderful organization of over 500 bereaved Israeli and Palestinians, all of whom have lost a family member in the conflict, seeks to serve as an important bridge towards peace and reconciliation in the region. [97]

ONE WORLD, ONE VISION, ONE VOICE

RESTORING FAITH IN OURSELVES

Someone said to me: "We are the ones we have been waiting for." This is so deeply connected to becoming conscious and responsible citizens of the world. Let's embrace the interconnectedness of our world , see its beauty, stand together and look for a vision that unites us.

The following paragraphs are from a review of *Planetary Citizenship: Your Values, Beliefs, and Actions Can Shape a Sustainable World*, a book by Hazel Henderson and Daisaku Ikeda, which is on the Middleway Press website (*www.middlewaypress.com*):

> Two world-renowned global activists [Henderson and Ike-da] explore the rise of "grassroots globalists"—citizens all over the world who are taking responsibility for building a more peaceful, harmonious and sustainable future. The authors also discuss their own backgrounds and what led them individually to activism on a worldwide scale. At the same time, they provide encouragement and concrete information for the millions of other concerned citizens who want to make a difference.
>
> A wide variety of issues that are now gaining greater recognition at all levels of society are explored, including

sustainable development, economic justice, respect for indigenous peoples and their traditional lands and resources, democratizing politics and international institutions, making corporations accountable, and conserving the Earth's biodiversity, water, air quality and climate.

Rather than dwell only on doom and gloom prophecies, Henderson and Ikeda embrace a practical yet profound optimism in human potential and our ability to build a brighter future. Arguing that a positive change of heart in one person can lead to a change in the world as a whole, they present compelling insights that will move and challenge the reader. By focusing on the spiritual values necessary to construct a better world, the two link complex global issues to ordinary people and assure us that we have the power to make a positive difference in our families, communities, countries, and the world at large.[98]

What a beautiful term: planetary citizen. There are quite a number of great organizations that actively work on resolving the issues we face as a humanity. They all act in the consciousness of planetary citizenship. We should not underestimate their influence. Here are a few:

The Earth Charter, launched in 2000, is an international declaration of fundamental values and principles considered useful by its supporters for building a just, sustainable, and peaceful global society in the 21st century. Created through a global consultation process, and endorsed by organizations representing millions of people, the charter "seeks to inspire in all peoples a sense of global interdependence and shared responsibility for the well-being of the human family, the greater community of life, and future generations." (*www.earthcharterinaction.org*)

The World Future Council (WFC) consists of up to 50 respected personalities from all five continents. They come from governments, parliaments, the arts, civil society, science, and the business world. Together, they form a voice for the rights of future generations. The World Future

Council Foundation is a charity registered in Hamburg, Germany, where its head office is located. Additionally, they have staff working in Brussels, London, Washington, and Johannesberg. (*www.worldfuturecouncil.org*)

The Global Marshall Plan was first suggested by then-senator Al Gore in 1992 in his bestselling book *Earth in the Balance: Ecology and the Human Spirit*, which gives specific ideas on how to save the global environment. The Global Marshall Plan (*www.globalmarshallplan.org*) was founded in 2003. Gore states in his book:

> The new plan will require the wealthy nations to allocate money for transferring environmentally helpful technologies to the Third World and to help impoverished nations achieve a stable population and a new pattern of sustainable economic progress. To work, however, any such effort will also require wealthy nations to make a transition themselves that will be in some ways more wrenching than that of the Third World.

The Club of Rome is an independent, not for profit global think tank that deals with a variety of international political issues. It was founded in April 1968 by a small international group of professionals and raised considerable public attention in 1972 with its report "The Limits to Growth." Its essential mission is "to act as a global catalyst for change through the identification and analysis of the crucial problems facing humanity and the communication of such problems to the most important public and private decision makers as well as to the general public." It contributed to the development of the concept of sustainability, which played an important role in highlighting the interdependence of environment and economics. (*www.clubofrome.org*)

The Forum 2000 Foundation aims to identify the key issues facing civilization and to explore ways in which to prevent escalation of conflicts that have religion, culture, or ethnicity as their primary components. It aims to provide a platform to discuss these important topics openly and to enhance global dialogue. Through their activities, it also intends to promote democracy in nondemocratic countries and to support the civil society; respect for human rights; and religious, cultural, and ethnic tolerance in young democracies. The Forum 2000 Foundation was founded in 1996 as a joint initiative of Czech President Václav Havel, Japanese philanthropist Yohei Sasakawa, and Nobel Peace Prize laureate Elie Wiesel. (*www.forum2000.cz*)

The WorldShift Network, Club of Budapest is also a founding member of the Global Marshall Plan. On June 12, 2007, the day of Professor Ervin Laszlo's 75th birthday, the Club of Budapest's WorldShift Network was established as an international foundation. The purpose of the foundation is to connect the multitude of organizations and individuals throughout the world already working for a value-based new civilization in order to strengthen their concerted political effectiveness in civil society. The founders are Prof. Ervin Laszlo (president), Johannes Heimrath, and Wolfgang Riehn (chairmen). (*www.worldshiftnetwork.org*)

The Caux Round Table (CRT) is an international organization of senior business executives aiming to promote ethical business practices. The Caux Round Table was founded in 1986 by Frederick Phillips, former president of Philips Electronics and Olivier Giscard d'Estaing, former Vice-Chairman of INSEAD, as a means of reducing escalating trade tensions. The CRT advocates implementation of the CRT Principles for Business through which principled capitalism can flourish and sustainable and socially responsible prosperity can become the foundation for a fair, free and transparent global society. (*www.cauxroundtable.org*)

CASSE, Center for the Advancement of Steady State Economy. The mission of CASSE is to advance the steady state economy, with stabilized population and consumption, as a policy goal with widespread public support. Conventional economists tend to overlook physical and ecological principles when considering the effects of economic growth. These economists, along with politicians, business leaders, the media, and the public at large, are not seeing the big picture when it comes to economic growth. That's where CASSE steps in. Their role is to help people understand the truth that growth isn't the answer to all our problems. Perpetual economic growth is neither possible nor desirable. Growth, especially in wealthy nations, is already causing more problems than it solves. They have created a fascinating report called "Enough Is Enough." (*www.steadystate.org*)

Money is such a common denominator for us all. The issues, problems, and joys in our life with money are so similar for everyone on Earth that it binds us together into one world. We all need to deal with money every day and because the basic financial and economic principles are so similar in many countries, we do exist in one world, can use one vision, and can raise one voice. In this togetherness, as planetary citizens, we can work toward the creation of a sustainable foundation for the future of economics and finance.

We need to believe in the shift, in ourselves and in each other, and believe that we can make this transition. We are on a threshold as humanity. A call for action and to work together lies deep in my heart.

I give thanks to all my colleagues and the angelic realms supporting me. Today (Nov 26, 2010) is the last day at Ocean Sands Beach Inn Hotel. I am completing the 21st chapter and just created a cover idea for the book. All went according to plan. Hazel and I have said our goodbyes. With her assistance, I gave birth to the whole book in 21 days. I want to give thanks to the beach and to the sea, which helped me to see a true dream. It is time for its reality and for the scales to tip towards living in the new world we envision.

One world, one vision, one voice.
When we look up at the sky can we see that one vision?
Can we hear the one voice in our hearts?
Are we existing in one world,
where we see the same path?

Together we can go through the door.
We can find the peace in our hearts
to relax with one another:
country by country, state by state,
person by person.

Creating a new financial system, a new economy, takes time.
What choice do we have, in the midst of our crisis,
but to listen to our hearts and go within
and find a new resourcefulness from the inside out.
We can unite in care. Let's dare to care.

Let's go toward world peace, to close the chapter.

To establish world peace
we need
to stand together,
respect one another,
and share.

Let's look at a world based on the Four Actions, as previously described in Chapter 2:

1. Embracing the gift together and receiving and sharing it.
2. Moving from ownership to stewardship.
3. Using money based on caring, sharing, loving, giving and receiving.
4. Moving from a money-first attitude to a care-first attitude.

We are on a threshold.
In a world created out of these four actions
There is no war
because we share the gift
and do not fight over it.

We need to choose.
In a world created out of these four actions
There is no hunger
because we share what is given to us all

We have a chance of making it.
In a world created out of these four actions
there is no pollution

because we respect, honor, and
do not harm the gift.

In that world
we understand that
we cannot own this planet and fight over what we think is ours.
We cannot take too much
while others do not have enough.
We cannot exploit or pollute the Earth.

I close with a poem about a caring, sharing, loving, giving, and receiving attitude with money:

When we receive,
all greed, fear, selfishness,
desire for power, and possessiveness heal.
When we share,
all of nature rejoices and we can see the meaning of life again.
When we give,
life smiles and money returns into its proper position.
When we love,
we create heaven on Earth.
When we care,
all bodies heal.

EPILOGUE:
LEARNING FROM NATURE

When we let our hearts speak, dreams can happen. They happen because of our imagination, perseverance, and commitment. An important key is to let our thinking be guided by our hearts. When the Condor (heart) and Eagle (head) fly together there will be Peace on Earth.

Gandhi said: "There is enough for our need, not for our greed." We need to rebalance ourselves. Our greed disturbs the natural balance of things; it disrupts the space and the fabric of our common humanity. We need to learn to manage our resources and divide them fairly.

From *The Money Fix* video at *www.ethicalmarkets.tv*, here are few more quotes by permaculture ecologist Scott Pittman, as he stands by a fir tree in the forest, explaining to a friend how nature deals with its resources:

> Whenever it rains, the rain directs a certain amount of the rainfall to the bark. The bark is set up into these elaborate patterns, to direct rain all the way around the tree and into the crevices where bugs, ants, and other critters live; a lot of exoskeletons [of insects, etc.] are shed here. They are dissolved by the rainwater, which runs down the tree and carries the phosphates from the bugs and their manure to the soil at the bottom of the tree. All this organic material in the soil is what feeds the tree. It's like a constant recycling of the material of life back into life.
>
> Here you have a kind of banking of resources, that every element in the forest contributes to. It's more like a community of contributors; and you take what you need as you need it. So there is this bank of resources at the bottom of that fir tree, which is available to the tree, the fungi, to the

earthworms and to termites, to whatever comes along and needs it; and each time someone takes something, they generally contribute something. There is not that kind profit motive or interest in natural systems. It really is not necessary to have more than you need, unless somehow you are inculturated to that belief system. There is a kind of scarcity boogie-bear in human culture that always has us feeling as if there is not enough or there is not going to be enough. We've got to quickly gather as much as we can and store it, where no one can get to it, and steal it from us, or rob us, and then it doesn't even matter if we really use it. [99]

Another quote from the *Money Fix* is by the evolutionary biologist Elisabet F. Sahtouris:

I don't think economics is related only to humans at all. It is very easy to see nature as an economy. Nature creates value constantly for the benefit of all its membership and that is what I think economics are really all about.

Charles Eisenstein, writer, speaker, and the author of *The Ascent of Humanity* [100] in his article "A Circle of Gifts" says,

Community is woven from gifts. Unlike today's market system, whose built-in scarcity compels competition in which more for me is less for you, in a gift economy the opposite holds. Because people in a gift culture pass on their surplus rather than accumulating it, your good fortune is my good fortune: more for you is more for me. Wealth circulates, gravitating toward the greatest need. In a gift community, people know that their gifts will eventually come back to them, albeit often in a new form. [101]

I can't stress enough that working together is our key. When we connect and work together, we can turn the tides. When we know that we are not dependent upon, or victimized by, the systems in our outer world, but have created them, we can replace and redesign them. We can come to new agreements about the design and functionality of our world economy and exchange systems. The good thing is that, in money matters, our needs are very similar and so is our sense of community. It is a field where agreement is possible. Even today, in our difficult times, we are operating our economy and financial worlds through agreed mechanisms we all work with. Therefore, let us work together as a world community and use this book and our online opportunities, as the platform to share our thoughts and ideas. *As nature demonstrates, by working together, we can do it!*

TAKING STEPS FORWARD

Establishing a new foundation for economics and finance worldwide to me is the same as the incarnation of a heart that guides all humanity. That heart is the key; we need to remind ourselves of this simple fact. This heart can guide humanity in the right direction and will give humanity all the answers it needs.

Dare to Care is intended to create a platform and be a resource for rethinking our economic and financial worlds and letting them be guided by this heart. It displays a set of possibilities and examples of what happens when we use this heart. The problem with our world is that we think we can do it without this heart, that we can make things work without love by just making shrewd business plans to serve ourselves and others, in which we can make things happen without too much warmth and care. The money-first world, where we use money at the expense of, instead of in service to, our values, well-being, and passions, does not anchor this heart.

In order to make this heart real in our lives, we almost need a new set of rules, or, to say it differently, we need to be obedient to certain natural laws. These laws are reflected through most religions when we return to the purity of their original teachings, simple truths like caring for one another, creating equality among all, loving everyone equally, and giving everyone the same space. Using this as a foundation, we all make our unique contributions as if to a huge painting, to which we all and add our specific color and shape, where we operate as nature does and we find true common ground, based on the freedom of love in the heart.

This heart needs to be called on by humanity to save itself from collapse and destruction. We know how violent our world still is. At the same time, many seeds of hope are sprouting to guide us forward onto a much brighter path. When we dare to care, we take action. We are opening up a space for change. For all of you who have read the book, we have created a proposal for cooperation, for joining our think tank, and working toward establishing that foundation together.

We invite you to participate in the seven levels of transformation, according to your own needs and aspirations. These are actions we can take individually and collectively:

> LEVEL 1: DEEP TRANSFORMATION. You can request the workshop "Meeting the Mystery of Money" and any other transformational work we do and ask for individual assistance. (There is more information on our website at *www.CareFirstWorld.com*.)

> LEVEL 2: TEAMWORK. Create or join a team, focused on a particular subject or issue, on any aspect of the transformation. When you feel you would like to be more involved and want to let your voice be heard, do let us know and you can become a part of the teamwork we are organizing. This book is only a beginning to get us started. Let's join our passions and move forward together. Would you like to start a team? Do you have something you want to work on? Who would you like to work with? How would you like to work together with others? We are happy to facilitate this process and help you to come in contact with others, wherever we can. We can integrate your impulse into our network and let others in the network know what you are doing.

> LEVEL 3: CONNECTING THE TEAMS—ESTABLISHING A WIDER NETWORK. We'll inform you what is happening in the whole network and give you ways to contact other teams when you want to exchange information or work together.

> LEVEL 4: ACTION—RAISING OUR POLITICAL VOICE. We can explore our involvement in politics where

needed, on a local, national, or international level, raising the cause—this can be the result of findings within the teams.

LEVEL 5: ACTUALIZATION—WORKING TOWARD CHANGES IN OUR LAWS AND REGULATIONS. This can evolve from the teamwork and political involvement.

LEVEL 6: WALKING OUR TALK—STARTING PROJ-ECTS AND INITIATIVES. When you want to start an initiative or project and wish to find out whether others are interested as well, you can present your suggestions on our online platform with your contact information and others can find you there.

LEVEL 7: A NEW EARTH—OUR END GOAL. This is the place we all aim for, work for, and would like to arrive at. The focus of all these levels is creating the new Earth and working toward establishing world peace. We can implement the seven levels of transformation. By utilizing them, we find more expression, show who we really are, and make our concerns and ideas more visible.

Could it be that our true purpose in life is to create that new Earth together, to play our humble role on this planet in the huge expanse of stars and galaxies? We may become a shining example of what people can do when they decide that love is the action, care the foundation, and sharing the way. We may be able to see what happens when humanity decides to give and receive with great fluidity and in service to all living systems in nature and when we say: "The Garden is the way, the place to return to, and the beginning of all; where we create a love-based economy and a care-first world for all children, people, animals, plants, and for our mineral kingdom."

CREATING OUR ONLINE PLATFORM

We are establishing an online interactive platform to facilitate the above and more. We also want anyone to be able to make contributions to our process anonymously, if they so choose. We might even use the chapters of the book as discussion forums and invite experts to speak about the different subjects we address. We want to make space for all our voices and all levels of participation. This is an attempt to see whether together, on a worldwide scale, we can create the economic and financial reality we desire. We see it as place where we can gather, develop, and access tools to build a love-based economy, a care-first world, and the Garden.

One of the most important changes to make, as I shared throughout the book, is that we all do the work we love. The importance of work is that it enables us to express what we are here to do, why we came to this Earth, and how we choose to serve. People who can do this are happy. We want to create a network, a possibility to meet online and in real life, where we assist one another to find our purpose, to connect, to do what we want and to work together, each one of us making our unique contribution.

We can hold council about world issues to let all of us create the destiny of this planet together; to let us be in communication about these issues and to connect to all initiatives and organizations that are doing the same. It is a bit like Google or Wikipedia, in the sense that we create an online and real-life platform to become a resource for this change and a facilitator of the change, a place where we can unite our efforts to create a new foundation for finance and economics together for generations to come.

We would like to take responsibility for coordinating this change as it emerges from within us and as it slowly moves into the areas of worldwide decision-making bodies and the world of political activity. We are not here to convert anyone to what we believe to be true. We are here to share and build together. *We invite everyone who wishes to respond to the book to join our think tank and let us know what your feelings, ideas, proposals, initiatives, and ventures are, as well as the needs that you might have.*

We have created an e-mail address (daretocare@carefirstworld.com), which can be used to connect with us and to respond to any of the above invitations. We can be in touch by phone, Skype, and through our online platform. Just let us know what you are looking for, and feel welcomed. We would love to hear your responses, and have your involvement, and we look forward to working together.

ACKNOWLEDGMENTS

My thanks go to Hazel Henderson, who so kindly gave me three weeks of her time and constant attention toward the writing of the book, and made her whole library available to me. Also to her husband, Alan F. Kay, who welcomed me into their home, and to her executive director, Rosalinda Sanquiche, for her support and advice throughout the process. *Dare to Care* developed out of the many passionate conversations between Hazel and myself. She is a great source of inspiration and my cheerleader in the writing of this book. Thank you, Hazel, for your profound commitment to the cause and to our shared focus.

Ernie Robson, from Washington, DC, assisted me with bringing the book more into focus. He contributed some of his own writing on finance and economics, and helped with his editing skills. We are creating an online platform together with others to start a conversation and stimulate worldwide cooperation on how we can create a love-based foundation for finance and for our economies for generations to come. We extend an invitation to the readers of the book and to the experts and all who wish to participate. Thank you for those great contributions.

We also want to thank Philip De Hudy for assisting us with his economic research.

It has been the unending support of my wife, Sandra Böhtlingk, which has upheld me through many tribulations and processes to come to the language of the heart in finance and economics. Sandra and I live what we speak of and she is the living example of what I dream for us all. Her courageous and wise presence envelops all who are near her, and I am honored to be in the presence of this every second of the day. Thank you for being in my life.

Gabriella Kapfer, from the United Kingdom, with whom Sandra and I run one of our companies, CareFirstWorld Ltd., has brought so much light into people's lives through living the dream and applying the principles we share. She blesses the world as a singer/musician and sound weaver, lifting us all into a space of empowerment and connection with self.[102] Thank you, my dearest friend and colleague.

I deeply thank everyone who has been previewing the book and assisting me with editing, comments, and the shaping of the book. My many thanks to John Steiner, Kenneth and Lois Leeb, Steve Schueth, Ruth Turner, and John Zwerver from the United States; Jon Freeman and Quentin Cowen from the UK; and Martha Reijnders, Brian Gude, Sue van Eesteren and Thierry de Wijn from the Netherlands.

I also want to particularly acknowledge my dear friend Jon Freeman from the United Kingdom, who has been passionately supporting me to share our vision on a much larger scale, and who wrote his 2010 book *Future Money—The Way We Survive Global Bankruptcy* to complement and support this book.

I want to acknowledge two members of our advisory board, my dear friends John Steiner and Steve Schueth, who have given me their constant support throughout the years at all different stages of the work. There are so many others have done the same: believing in me and encouraging me to continue building a vision that clearly was a common dream, but of which the application was underway and in process.

The vision I share with you, dear reader, has formed itself through the active involvement of hundreds of these colleagues and friends. We have processed the concepts and brought them into reality by applying them in our individual and communal lives since 1989. I honor them all and would like to acknowledge them here: Stanley Messenger, Gudrun Pelham, Elana Freeman, Rob and Jehanne Metha, and Heather Cowen from the United Kingdom; David and Aslaug Brittaine from Norway; David Kapfer from Germany; Harry and Greetje Raven and Gerda Berend from the Netherlands.

Also the many friends from the United States: Patty Snyder, Airisun Wonderli, and Eric Thompson, from Virginia; Makasha and Katherine Roske, Marie and Richard Ruster, Dabo and Linda Fisher from New Mexico; Logon Kline, Travis Robinson, Bud Wilson, Candice Powers, Sky

Canyon, James Plagmann, Bill Carpenter, and Linda Sue Shirkey from Colorado; Devin Mikles, Rob and Trina Brunk, Toni Hosseini, Forrist Lytehaause, Bill Kauth, and Marz Attar from other states. I also want to thank Deborah Cameron from Canada.

There are many more, and together we've helped to build each other's lives. I hope this will continue with many others to come through the process of this book and what we hope to achieve.

NOTES

FOREWORD

1   According to Google, "PageRank reflects our view of the importance of web pages by considering more than 500 million variables and 2 billion terms. Pages that we believe are important pages receive a higher PageRank and are more likely to appear at the top of the search results." Source: article on PageRank at *en.wikipedia.org/wiki/PageRank* (accessed July 20, 2010). When you do a search for anything, Google has an algorithmic method of determining what comes first on the search page. With a website like www.ethicalmarkets.com, if anyone searches the term *ethical markets* it comes up first because it has one of the few urls with those key words, because it is currently an active site with lots of pages, because it has a high Google PageRank, etc.

2   Hazel Henderson explains, "Ethical Markets Media (USA and Brazil) as an independent multi-media social enterprise does not grow. Cancer cells grow. The code of life, DNA, does not grow, it replicates. We replicate our content (cultural DNA) worldwide, which allows us to stay small. Small is beautiful, as one of our great mentors, E. F. Schumacher taught."

INTRODUCTION

3   From Peter Blom's article "Sustaining Sustainability" in *Triodos News*, Summer 2008, Edition 30.

4   To order *Future Money* go to *www.freemanj.com/spiralworld/products/* (accessed July 14, 2011).

5   Jon Freeman, from *Future Money* Chapter 13.

OUR PERSONAL STORY

6   You can order *Money Is Love* at: *www.barbarawilder.com/pages/MoneyIsLove. html* (accessed July 14, 2011).

7   Jon Freeman, *Future Money,* Chapter 13.

CHAPTER 1

8   See www.hazelhenderson.com, where you see can see a wonderful profile of Hazel by Nathalie Beekman (accessed July 14, 2011).

CHAPTER 2

9   I decided to use the words, because I feel they convey the essence of a message so clearly and beautifully and I would like to use them just for their truth although I am aware of the fact that the historical validity of this speech is in question. In an article "Thus Spoke Chief Seattle: The Story of an Undocumented Speech" by Jerry L. Clark, he says: "The words of this Indian spokesman have been frequently quoted to a wide audience via the newspaper and television media. The Smithsonian's Nation of Nations exhibit includes a portion of Seattle's supposed speech for the benefit of the thousands of tourists who visit our nation's capital each year. Despite its popularity, this affirmation of Indian eloquence may not be founded in historical reality." (see *Prologue Magazine,* Spring 1985, Vol. 18 (1), *www. archives.gov/publications/prologue/1985/spring/chief-seattle.html.*)

10   Jon Freeman, *Future Money,* Chapter 13.

11   Jon Freeman, *Future Money,* Chapter 13.

12   Jon Freeman, *Future Money,* Chapter 13.

13   Jon Freeman, *Future Money,* Chapter 13.

14   Jon Freeman, *Future Money,* Chapter 13.

CHAPTER 3

15   The four-dimensional cake is from Hazel Henderson's video profile at *www. hazelhenderson.com* (accessed July 14, 2011).

16   Riane Eisler, *The Real Wealth of Nations: Creating a Caring Economics,* Berrett-Koehler, 2007.

17   Riane Eisler, *The Real Wealth of Nations,* page 13.

18   The gross domestic product (GDP) or gross domestic income (GDI) is the market value of all final goods and services made within the borders of a

country in a given year. It is often an indicator of the standard of living. (from Wikipedia article on "Gross Domestic Product"), *en.wikipedia.org/ wiki/Gross_domestic_product* (accessed July 14, 2011).

19 Gross National Product (GNP) is the market value of all goods and services produced in one year by labor and property supplied by the residents of a country. Unlike Gross Domestic Product (GDP), which defines production based on the geographical location of production, GNP includes net production based on ownership. It includes income from remittances from abroad. From Wikipedia article "Gross National Product," *en.wikipedia.org/ wiki/Gross_national_product* (accessed July 14, 2011).

20 Judith Schwartz's article, "Is GDP an Obsolete Measure of Progress?" is at *www.time.com/time/business/article/0,8599,1957746,00.html* (accessed July 14, 2011).

21 Re "GDP Fetishism" see article "GDP Fetishism" Sept 2009 by Joseph Stiglitz at *folk.uio.no/sholden/E1310/gdp-fetishism-stiglitz.pdf*. David Henderson also wrote about it in his article with the same title "GDP Fetishism" March 2010. See: *econlog.econlib.org/archives/2010/03/ gdp_fetishism.html*. David says: "GDP has become the Holy Grail. GDP has replaced well-being. That's GDP fetishism." He also says: "When economics professors teach the basics of Gross Domestic Product (GDP), we usually caution our students that it is not a good measure of welfare. Unfortunately, many economists go on to give GDP far more credit than it deserves. They tend to consider fiscal and monetary policy positive if these policies increase GDP, but they often fail to ask, let alone answer, whether those same policies increase or reduce welfare. I have a term for giving GDP such a sacred a place in economists' reasoning: GDP fetishism. If we return to some basic principles of economics, we will avoid GDP fetishism, do better economic analysis, and propose better policies." (Both sites accessed July 14, 2011.)

22 Also not measured in GDP is: the state of the environment; the quality of our soil, water, and air, and the effect of climate change.

23 For more information about the Quality of Life Indicators, see the Overview section of www.calvert-henderson.com at *www.calvert-henderson. com/Overview-why12.htm* (accessed July 14, 2011).

24 The report "State of Society: Measuring Economic Success and Human Well-Being" was written by Erwin de Leon and Elizabeth T. Boris,

published by the Urban Institute Center on Nonprofits and Philanthropy, 2010. *www.urban.org.*

CHAPTER 4

25 See Jon Freeman, *Future Money,* Chapter 4.

26 The idea of right livelihood is an ancient one. It embodies the principle that each person should follow an honest occupation, which fully respects other people and the natural world. It means being responsible for the consequences of our actions and taking only a fair share of the earth's resources. (*www.rightlivelihood.org/right livelihood.html* (accessed July 14, 2011).

27 Desmond Tutu on You Tube on Basic Income (November 8, 2006), *www.youtube.com/watch?v=gf3n-L5FDy0* (accessed July 7, 2011).

28 The Universal Declaration of Human Rights can be found at *www.un.org/en/documents/udhr/index.shtml#a2.5*

CHAPTER 5

29 Watch John Perkins video from May 2008 at: *www.vimeo.com/4107173* (accessed July 14, 2011).

CHAPTER 6

30 Quoted from *The Co-Creator's Handbook* by Carolyn Anderson with Katharine Roske.

31 Quoted from *www.globalincome.org/English/BI-worldwide.html* (accessed July 14, 2011).

32 *www.globalincome.org/English/BI-worldwide.html* (accessed July 15, 2011).

33 The Götz Werner quote is from an article titled "A Basic Income: a Basis for The Future." See *www.unternimm-die-zukunft.de/?id=76* under "English texts" (accessed July 14. 2011).

34 From the first part of the speech. Full PDF version is available at: *www.un.org/ga/econcrisissummit/statements/pga_opening_en.pdf* (accessed July 14, 2011).

CHAPTER 7

35 From the last part of Miguel D'Escoto-Brockmann's UN speech. Full PDF version is at *www.un.org/ga/econcrisissummit/statements/pga_opening_en.pdf* (accessed, July 14 2011).

CHAPTER 8

36 Page 2 of *Beyond Globalization: Shaping a Sustainable Global Economy*, by Hazel Henderson.

37 Page 4 of *Beyond Globalization: Shaping a Sustainable Global Economy*, by Hazel Henderson.

38 Page 4 of *Beyond Globalization: Shaping a Sustainable Global Economy*, by Hazel Henderson.

39 Page 38 of *Beyond Globalization: Shaping a Sustainable Global Economy*, by Hazel Henderson.

CHAPTER 11

40 Money as information quote is from *www.ethicalmarkets.tv/video-show/?v=88 Re-designing Money Systems to Reduce Greenhouse Gases and Accelerate the Growing Green Economy,* video 191 (accessed July 14, 2011).

41 "Blessed are you who are poor, for yours is the kingdom of God." Quote is from Luke 6:20, New International Version.

42 And elsewhere in the Bible, Christ says "The kingdom of Heaven is within you." Matthew 5:3 has it more accurately, as "Blessed are the poor in spirit, for theirs is the kingdom of Heaven." The original Greek word interpreted as "spirit" is *pneumati,* which also means "breath." Modern science has shown us that when one experiences higher states of consciousness called "transcendence" or "satori," there is a marked drop in oxygen fconsumption, as much as twice as great a drop as we experience in deep sleep. So Christ was most likely describing the experience of "transcendence" and its accompanying refinement of breath and inner peace and bliss, not admonishing us to become poor or stay poor as the path to Heaven.

43 "A Path To Downward Mobility," by Robert J. Samuelson, October 13, 2009 at *www.newsweek.com/2009/10/13/a-path-to-downward-mobility.html* (accessed July 20, 2011).

44 "Multiple Welfare Exits and Recidivism: Understanding Culture of Poverty, Local Labor Market /Area Characteristics, Job Quality and Welfare Reform," by Ini Choi Shin, Case Western Reserve University, Cleveland, Ohio at *https://kb.osu.edu/dspace/bitstream/handle/1811/37364/17_shin_paper.pdf* (accessed July 20, 2011).

45 The Obama Administration's FY 2012 budget request to the Internal Revenue Service is nearly $13.3 billion: see IRS FY 2012 Budget Proposal

Summary at *www.irs.gov/newsroom/article/0,,id=235959,00.html* (accessed July 20, 2011).

46 Zachary Roth, "Chart Shows Low Tax Burden for Rich," Yahoo, March 16, 2011 at *news.yahoo.com/s/yblog_thelookout/20110316/ts_yblog_thelookout/chart-shows-low-tax-burden-for-rich* (accessed July 20, 2011).

47 Niklas Pollard, "UN Report Puts World's Illicit Drug Trade at Estimated $321b," June 30, 2005 at Boston.com (*The Boston Globe*), *www.boston.com/news/world/europe/articles/2005/06/30/un_report_puts_worlds_illicit_drug_trade_at_estimated_321b/* (accessed July 20, 2011).

48 About cowry shells, see article "Cowry" on Wikipedia at *en.wikipedia.org/wiki/Cowry#Human_use* (accessed July 20, 2011).

49 See John G. Gurley and Edward S. Shaw, "Money," in *American Economic History*, edited by Seymour E. Harris (New York: McGraw Hill, 1961). The commodities market allows sellers of grain, for example, to be sure what price they will get in the future for their product. Buyers such as bread-making companies can be sure of what their longer-term costs of production will be. Even speculators help by providing liquidity and market discovery, which identify the balance at supply-and-demand intersection points.

50 The movie *Inside Job* was written and directed by Charles Ferguson (Sony Pictures Classics, 2010). The "biggest bank heist in our history" appears around 01:14:45.00 in the documentary. Around 01:40:16.29, they specifically talk about the finance industry knowing how risky their decisions were, but not caring.

51 The video is at Ellen Brown's website called the *Web of Debt*, *www.webofdebt.com/media/eb1.php* (accessed July 20, 2011).

52 Fannie Mae is the nickname of FNMA, the Federal National Mortgage Association (*www.fanniemae.com*), established 1938. Ginnie Mae is the nickname of GNMA, the Government National Mortgage Association (*www.ginniemae.gov*), established 1968. Freddie Mac is the nickname of the FHLMC, the Federal Home Loan Mortgage Association, established 1970 (*www.freddiemac.gov*). These government-sponsored enterprises (GSEs) were established to provide liquidity in the housing mortgage markets and for other public purposes. This was initially done through the banking system via loans. During the Vietnam war, in 1968, President Lyndon Johnson privatized Fannie Mae to remove it from the federal government's balance

sheet and created another quasi-private company, the Federal Home Loan Mortgage Corporation, known as Freddie Mac, which would deal with the savings banks. By 1980, they were encouraged to compete against each other (see *www.csmonitor.com/USA/Politics/2011/0211/Fannie-Mae-and-Freddie-Mac-101-How-much-will-we-miss-them*). So it can be said that the direct predecessors to CDOs were the earliest mortgage-backed securities (or MBSs), created in 1968 at Ginnie Mae, in 1971 at Freddie Mac, and 1981 at Fannie Mae. From small and humble beginnings, these institutions became the giants of the US mortgage industry. From the 1980s and 1990s, these institutions greatly expanded until today in 2011 they own or guarantee over half (57%) of the $12 trillion US mortgage market. As of September 2008, these institutions were put into conservatorship under the Federal Housing Finance Agency.

53 CDO information from *en.wikipedia.org/wiki/Collateralized_debt_obligation* (accessed Sept 20, 2011).

54 It is pretty well agreed that one of the major causes of the Great Depression was a sharp contraction in the money supply in the short run, and the length of the Depression was also at least in part due to the inability of countries to expand the supply of money while remaining on the "gold standard" (see Wikipedia article, "The Great Depression," *en.wikipedia.org/wiki/Great_Depression#Gold_standard*). In fact, by 1932, most major countries had abandoned the gold standard. However, the money supply was not the only cause of the Great Depression. It turns out, in hindsight, that the Great Depression was, like our recent major financial crisis of 2007–2009, the perfect storm, where many bad things, created by many different forces, and driven by human greed and folly, drove the world's economies to the brink of collapse.

55 It is important to note that although the structure of many of these mortgages was predatory, and the marketing practices to get homeowners to refinance were also predatory, the sale of mortgages also gave rise to high originating fees. This focused on immediate profit for the loan originators instead of long-term viability of the mortgage.

56 Insiders like the CEO of Goldman Sachs who presided over this dubious activity were making over $450 million a year in salaries and bonuses. Ultimately, we know that in the process of cleaning up this mess and restoring order to the financial system, middle-class taxpayers in the United States paid

for this compensation. No one, not even a jury of their CEO peers, would agree $450 million was a reasonable compensation for the efforts of the CEOs of financial institutions. It was a throwback to the days where the chief pirate got a bigger share of the booty and plunder than his crew. Even a jury of elementary school children would see the inherent wrongness in the CEOs' behavior and in their institution's behavior, which created the crisis.

57   Bearn Stearns, like many other financial institutions, also had very little equity, as they were buying these CDOs with a reserve ratio of less than 3 cents on the dollar, a 35-to-1 leverage. They were financing this with short-term loans from the overnight money markets. Eventually they were caught, when they could get no more short-term money. On a historical note, this behavior (borrowing in the short-term to finance a long-term asset like a 20- to 30-year mortgage was the same behavior that caused the collapse of the US Savings and Loan industry in the 1980s and 1990s.

58   You can see Public Law 111 at *www.gpo.gov/fdsys/pkg/PLAW-111publ203/content-detail.html*.

59   You can see H.R. 4173 at *www.govtrack.us/congress/billxpd?bill=h111-4173* (accessed July 11, 2011).

60   Note: The Dodd-Frank Act was a product of the financial regulatory reform agenda of the Democratically controlled 111th United States Congress and was based on proposed legislation from the Obama administration.

Wikipedia, in its overview, states: "The Act is categorized into sixteen titles and by one law firm's count, it requires that regulators create 243 rules, conduct 67 studies, and issue 22 periodic reports. The stated aim of the legislation is: To promote the financial stability of the United States by improving accountability and transparency in the financial system, to end "too big to fail," to protect the American taxpayer by ending bailouts, to protect consumers from abusive financial services practices, and . . . other purposes. Details of the act can be seen at: Dodd-Frank Wall Street Reform and Consumer Protection Act en.wikipedia.org/wiki/Dodd-Frank_Wall_Street_Reform_and_Consumer_Protection_Act (accessed July 20, 2011).

61   The Emergency Economic Stabilization Act of 2008 (HR 1424) may be seen at *www.govtrack.us/congress/bill.xpd?bill=h110-1424*. See also article, The Emergency Economic Stabilization Act of 2008, at *en.wikipedia.org/wiki/Emergency_Economic_Stabilization_Act_of_2008* (accessed July 6, 2011).

62 Re the similarities between environmental and financial regulation: Regulations and the institutions that enforce these regulations are not always helpful to consumers because the regulated industry often has the resources and motivation to legally manipulate the system. In the US natural gas pipelines, telecommunications, airlines, and railroads were all deregulated in the 1980s and 1990s, resulting in good for consumers. But, unlike the current financial system, all of these industries had multiple large financial and technological competitors, so in general the common consumer was served.

The success of deregulating power generation and distribution in the US was mixed. For example, Enron was able to manipulate derivatives and the deregulated electrical distribution system in California, which led to bankrupting California utilities. And it should be noted that environmental regulation has over time moved forward, with more integration with the principles of market economies, hence emissions trading, but all based on standards for the commons and on an understanding that there are many sources of pollution into the commons and some are inherently more easy to control than others.

In reregulating the global financial commons, we may well be surprised by a financial effect much like that seen by Michael E. Porter and Claas van der Linde in their work on environmental regulation, published in the September–October 1995 *Harvard Business Review* 73 (5) article "Green and Competitive: Ending the Stalemate." In their review of the article, the editors of the journal noted: "The authors' research shows that tougher environmental standards actually can enhance competitiveness by pushing companies to use resources more productively. Managers must start to recognize environmental improvement as an economic and competitive opportunity, not as an annoying cost or an inevitable threat. Environmental progress demands that companies innovate to raise resource productivity— precisely the new challenge of global competition."

However, in environmental regulation of the commons, there are still massive disconnects, which create environmental problems that remain unsolved. Mining and smelting, internal combustion, power generation, and recycling all are massive problems and are currently expensive failures of the regulation of our environmental commons.

Unfortunately, there are certain major industrialization and economic development processes in which no one has the economic power or incentive to invest to make these changes. Here innovative cooperation between regulators and the industries regulated and better integration to the financial system is necessary.

CHAPTER 13

63   From Peter Blom's article "Sustaining Sustainability" in *Triodos News,* Summer 2008, Edition 30.

64   From Peter Blom's article "A Bank That Connects People" in *Triodos News,* March 2009, Edition 34.

65   Information from *en.wikipedia.org/wiki/Grameen_Bank* (accessed July 14, 2011).

66   Information from *www.grameen-info.org/index.php?option=com_content&task=view&id=210&Itemid=379* (accessed July 14, 2011).

67   Information from *www.grameen-info.org/index.php?option=com_content&task=view&id=26&Itemid=0* (accessed July 14, 2011).

68   Historic information from *www.mondragon-corporation.com/ENG/Co-operativism/Co-operative-Experience/Historic-Background.aspx* (accessed July 14, 2011).

69   Mondragón information from *en.wikipedia.org/wiki/Mondrag%C3%B3n* (accessed July 14, 2011).

70   Peters quote is from *www.newswise.com/articles/view/17012* (accessed July 14, 2011).

71   Information on Roy Morrison's book about Mondragón is at: *www.beechriverbooks.com/id21.html* (accessed July 14, 2011).

72   Read more about ESOPs at *www.esopassociation.org* and *www.kelsoinstitute.org* (accessed July 14, 2011).

73   Patricia Aburdene's book is at *www.amazon.com/Megatrends-2010-Rise-Conscious-Capitalism/dp/1571744568* (accessed July 14, 2011).

74   Article "Conscious Business" is from *en.wikipedia.org/wiki/Conscious_business* (accessed July 14, 2011).

75   Quotes are from Conscious Capitalism Institute website, *www.cc-institute.com/cci/* (accessed July 14, 2011).

76   John Mackey's information is at *www.wholefoodsmarket.com/blogs/jmackey/2006/11/09-conscious-capitalism-creating-a-new-paradigm-for-business/* (accessed July 11, 2011).

CHAPTER 14

77   Interview with Götz Werner is at *www.oursystem.info/2010/04/basic-income-interview-with-gotz-werner.html* (accessed July 14, 2011).

CHAPTER 15

78   The definition of global commons is from *en.wikipedia.org/wiki/Global_commons* (accessed July 14, 2011).

79   From article "What Are Global Commons" on *www.wisegeek.com/what-are-global-commons.htm* (accessed July 17, 2011): The commons is a concept that has been used in many societies for centuries, usually when referring to land such as the village square or fields used for grazing livestock, that was not privately owned but belonged to the community as a whole. Global commons is a more recent concept, most often used in economics and politics, and usually refers to various natural resources and geographical areas, commonly including the deep sea bed, outer space, the oceans, the continent of Antarctica, and sometimes the entire Earth. These global commons are internationally shared resources and spaces that are not under the ownership or control of any state or person. Often, global commons are also defined as being necessary for human survival. The concept of global commons is most commonly used when debating environmental issues such as global warming and overfishing, and in discussions about how to implement and enforce laws to protect and manage these shared resources.

There is no universally accepted definition of what constitutes global commons. However, in an international report from 1980, backed by several international organizations, global commons are said to include the oceans, the atmosphere, "parts of the earth's surface beyond national jurisdictions," and Antarctica. The concept is sometimes broadened to include social, intellectual and cultural resources such as traditions, languages, and scientific knowledge.

80   See Daniel W. Bromley and Jeffrey Cochrane, "Understanding the Global Commons," Environmental and Natural Resources Training Project (EPAT/MUCIA). Working Paper 13, July 1994 at *www.aae.wisc.edu/pubs/misc/docs/em13.pdf* (accessed July 14, 2011).

81   re: Ethical Markets, see article "Financial Group Recognizes Finance as a Global Commons," dated September 13, 2010. To view and sign the petition go to *www.transformingfinance.net* and click on the link to "Full Statement and Signatories" (accessed July 17, 2011).

82 Read more about the history of Bretton Woods at *news.bbc.co.uk/2/ hi/7725157.stm* (accessed on July 16, 2011). I quote a small part of the article "How Bretton Woods Reshaped the World" by Steve Schifferes, November 14, 2008. "In the summer of 1944, delegates from 44 countries met in the midst of World War II to reshape the world's international financial system. . . . The meeting was part of the process led by the US to create a new international world order based on the rule of law, which also led to the creation of the United Nations and the strengthening of other international organisations. The delegates focused on two key issues: how to establish a stable system of exchange rates, and how to pay for rebuilding the war-damaged economies of Europe."

83 "Transforming Finance Group's Call Recognizes Finance as a Global Commons," at *www.ethicalmarkets.com/2010/09/12/transforming-finance-groups-call-recognizes-finance-as-a-global-commons*.

CHAPTER 16

84 Quote is from Ellen Brown's book, *Web of Debt,* page 478.

85 From Barbara Wilder's book *Money Is Love,* page 82.

86 Here is the definition of fractional reserve system (FRS) according to Business Dictionary.com, *www.businessdictionary.com/definition/fractional-reserve-system-FRS.html* (accessed July 14, 2011): "Monetary policy at the basis of the modern banking system. Under FRS, banks are required to hold only a fraction (typically 12 percent) of the depositors' funds as cash reserves. The remaining 88 percent of deposited funds can be loaned out to create new deposits which in turn create new loans . . . and so on, exerting a multiplier effect on the total money supply. However, in case of a bank run, this policy can cause banks to suffer huge losses and may even push them into bankruptcy."

87 For some more information on currency based on energy go to *www. theperfectcurrency.org/energy-currency.htm* (accessed July 14, 2011). It is also interesting to read an article by Hazel Henderson, "A Win-Win Plan for Iceland, Britain and the Netherlands," March 2010, *www.ethicalmarkets. com/2010/03/10/a-win-win-plan-for-iceland-britain-and-the-netherlands/* (accessed July 21, 2011).

CHAPTER 19

88 The full story of *The Man Who Planted Trees* by Jean Giono is at *www. arvindguptatoys.com/arvindgupta/plantedtrees.pdf* (accessed July 14, 2011).

89 The book review of *The Man Who Planted Trees* is at *www.doyletics.com/_arj1/ manwhopl.htm* (accessed July 14, 2011).

90 "Ryan's Well: How a 6-Year-Old Started Changing the World," by Ariella Ford, is at *life.gaiam.com/article/ryans-well-how-6-year-old-started-changing-world* (accessed July 14, 2011)

CHAPTER 20

91 Source of data is *www.myseniorportal.com/app/webroot/arthurdocs/socially_ responsible_investing.htm* (accessed July 14, 2011).

92 Statement is from Green America website, *www.greenamerica.org/* (accessed July 14, 2011).

93 Definition of fair trade is from article "Fair Trade" at *en.wikipedia.org/wiki/ Fair_trade* (accessed July 14, 2011).

94 Information about fair trade certification is from "Fair Trade Certification," at *en.wikipedia.org/wiki/Fairtrade_certification* (accessed July 14, 2011).

95 Information about Chris Mann is from *guayaki.com*; article "Guayaki becomes First Fair Trade-Certified Yerba Mate," by Timothy B. Hurst, April 21, 2009, at *eatdrinkbetter.com/2009/04/21/guayaki-becomes-first-fair-trade-certified-yerba-mate*; and interview at Tonic.com, "In the Hot Seat: Chris Mann" at *blog.tonic.com?s=guayaki+yerba+mate from May 3, 2010* (accessed July 14, 2011).

96 From Henderson, Hazel. *Ethical Markets: Growing the Green Economy,* page 96.

97 Information about Amber Chand is from the Women's Peace Collection website, *www.womenspeacecollection.com/gifts/jerusalem-candle-of-hope* (accessed July 6, 2011).

CHAPTER 21

98 Review of *Planetary Citizenship* is at *www.middlewaypress.com/planetary.html* (accessed July 6, 2011).

EPILOGUE

99 Quotes by Scott Pittman and Elisabet Sahtouris are from *The Money Fix* video by Alan Rosenblith and Hazel Henderson, distributed by *Ethical Markets TV.* It can be seen at *www.ethical markets.tv* (video 0333).

100 Read more about Charles Eisentein on *www.ascentofhumanity.com/* (accessed on July 14, 2011).

101 "A Circle of Gifts" by Charles Eisenstein is from *shareable.net/blog/charles-eisenstein-gift-economy-gift-circles* (accessed July 14, 2011).

ACKNOWLEDGMENTS

102 For more info about Gabriella's work see: *www.peace-trails.com* (accessed July 14, 2011).

BIBLIOGRAPHY

Aburdene, Patricia. *Megatrends 2010: The Rise of Conscious Capitalism.* Charlottesville: Hampton Roads Publishing Co., 2007.

Anderson, Carolyn and Katherine Roske. *The Co-Creator's Handbook: An Experiential Guide for Discovering Your Life's Purpose and Building a Co-creative Society.* Nevada City: Global Family, 2008.

Broere, Ad. *Een Menselijke Economie [A Human Economy].* Soesterberg: Uitgeverij Aspect, 2009.

Brown, Ellen Hodgson. *The Web of Debt: The Shocking Truth About Our Money System and How We Can Break Free.* Baton Rouge: Third Millennium Press 2010.

Brown, Lester. *Eco-Economy.* New York: W. W. Norton & Company, 2001.

Cahn, Edgar. *No More Throw-Away People: The Co-Production Imperative.* Washington, D. C.: Essential Books, 2000.

De Leon, Edwin, and Elizabeth T. Boris. *The State of Society: Measuring Economic Success and Human Well-Being.* Washington, D. C.: Urban Institute, 2010.

Eisler, Riane. *The Real Wealth of Nations.* San Franscisco: Berrett-Koehler Publishers, 2007.

Freeman, Jon. *Future Money: The Way We Survive Global Bankruptcy.* Ringwood: Spiralworld 2010.

Giono, Jean. *The Man Who Planted Trees.* White River Junction: Chelsea Green Publishing Co., 1985.

Gore, Al. *Earth in the Balance: Ecology and the Human Spirit.* Boston, Houghton Mifflin, 1992.

Henderson, Hazel. *Ethical Markets: Growing the Green Economy.* White River Junction: Chelsea Green Publishing Company, 2006.

Henderson, Hazel. *The Politics of The Solar Age: Alternatives to Economics.* Indianapolis: Knowledge Systems, 1988.

Henderson. Hazel. *Beyond Globalization: Shaping a Sustainable Global Economy.* West Hartford: Kumarian Press, 1999.

Henderson, Hazel, and Daisaku Ikeda. *Planetary Citizenship: Your Values, Beliefs, and Actions Can Shape a Sustainable World.* Santa Monica: Middleway Press, 2004.

Loye, David. *Darwin's Lost Theory.* Carmel: The Benjamin Franklin Press, 2007.

Lietaer, Bernard. *The Future of Money.* London: Century, Random House Ltd, 2001.

Morrison, Roy. *We Build the Road as We Travel: Mondragon: A Cooperative Social System.* Philadelphia: New Society Publishers, 1991.

Perkins, John. *Confessions of an Economic Hit Man.* San Franscisco: Berrett-Koehler Publishers, 2004.

Rosenblith, Alan, producer; Hazel Henderson, editor. *The Money Fix* (video), distributed by Ethical Markets TV 2008, filmed in different locations.

Schwartz, Judith. "Is GDP an Obsolete Measure of Progress?" *Time* Magazine, January 30, 2010.

Twist, Lynne. *The Soul of Money.* New York: W.W. Norton & Company, 2003.

Wilder, Barbara. *Money Is Love.* Boulder: Wild Ox Press, 1998.

KEY ORGANIZATIONS AND WEBSITES INVOLVED WITH THE TRANSFORMATION OF FINANCIAL SYSTEMS

BerkShares: Local Currency for the Berkshire Region, P.O. Box 125, Great Barrington, MA 01230, USA. Tel. +1(413) 528-1737 (*www. berkshares.org*)

BerkShares, co-sponsored by The New Economics Institute (*neweconomicsinstitute.org*), a US organization that uniquely combines vision, theory, action, and communication to effect a transition to a new economy—an economy that gives priority to supporting human well-being and Earth's natural systems.

BIEN: Basic Income Earth Network, c/o Chaire Hoover d'éthique économique et sociale, Université catholique de Louvain, Place Montesquieu, 3, B-1348 Louvain-la-Neuve, Belgium.(*www.basicincome.org/bien*)

BIEN aims to serve as a link between individuals and groups committed to, or interested in, basic income, i.e., an income unconditionally granted to all on an individual basis.

Calvert-Henderson Quality of Life Indicators, USA. (*www.calvert-henderson.com*)

The Calvert-Henderson Quality of Life Indicators are a contribution to the worldwide effort to develop comprehensive statistics of national well-being. The dimensions of life examined include: education, employment, energy, environment, health, human rights, income, infrastructure, national security, public safety, recreation and shelter.

Care First World Ltd., Mill Cottage, Letcoombe Bassett, Wantage, Oxfordshire OX12 9LL, UK. Tel. +44 (0) 1235 (*www.carefirstworld*.com)

It is the UK trading subsidiary of our Scottish charity, World Finance Initiative. This is the home address of Gabriella Kapfer, who founded the Company with us (Louis and Sandra Bohtlingk) in 2006. The best way to contact us through our website and our e-mail: daretocare@ carefirstworld.com.

Center for Partnership Studies, Co-founded by Riane Eisler and David Loye, California, USA. (*www.partnershipway.org*)

A nonprofit organization working to create a more peaceful, equitable and sustainable world through cultural transformation. The mission of the Center for Partnership Studies is to accelerate movement to partnership systems of gender and racial equity, economic prosperity, and a sustainable environment through research, education, grassroots empowerment, and policy initiatives that promote: Human development, social well-being, and long-term economic success, with special emphasis on valuing the work of caring and care-giving still primarily done by women.

Complementary Currency Resource Center, (*www.complementarycurrency.org*)

Resources for LETS (Local Exchange Trading Systems) and other *complementary currency* systems.

Conscious Capitalism, USA. (*www.consciouscapitalism.org*)

Conscious Capitalism is led by business leaders who are focused on using profit for a greater purpose. The Conscious Capitalism Institute does research and teaching and tries to promote a model of capitalism that is conscious and aligned with the interests of society, in which profitable businesses create multiple kinds of wealth and well-being.

The E. F. Schumacher Society, 140 Jug End Road, Great Barrington, MA 01230, USA. Tel. +1 (413) 528-1737 (*www.smallisbeautiful.org*)

A society that offers educational programs that seek to link people, land, and community by building local economies.

Ethical Markets Media, LLC, P.O Box 5190, St. Augustine, FL 32085, USA. Tel. +1 (904) 829-3140 (*www.ethicalmarkets.com*)

The executive director and contact person is Rosalinda Sanquiche. Founded by Hazel Henderson. It disseminates information on green investing, socially responsible investing, green business, green energy, business ethics news, etc. Here you will find information about the Green Transition Scoreboard.

The Fairtrade Foundation, 3rd Floor, Ibex House, 42-47 Minories, London EC3N 1DY, UK Tel. + 44 (0) 20-7405-5942 (*www.fairtrade.org.uk*)

Home of the Fairtrade Mark, the only independent guarantee of a better deal for Third World producers of agricultural products, cotton, gold, and more.

First Affirmative Financial Network, LLC, 2503 Walnut Street, Suite 201, Boulder, Colorado 80302, USA. Tel. +1 877-540-4933 (*www.firstaffirmative.com*)

A network of investment firms providing socially responsible investment management and administration for clients throughout the United States. Steven J. Schueth is President and Chief Marketing Officer of First Affirmative Financial Network.

The Global Alliance for Banking on Values, Nieuweroordweg 1, P.O. Box 55, 3700 AB Zeist, The Netherlands. Tel: +31 (0)30-694-2421 (*www.gabv.org*)

Thirteen banks who have joined together to form a new alliance in a move to build a positive alternative to the current crisis in the global financial system.

Global Ecovillage Network (GEN), (*gen.ecovillage.org*)

A growing network of sustainable communities and initiatives that bridge different cultures, countries, and continents.

Global Family, 11689 Lowhills Road, Nevada City, CA 95959, USA. Tel. +1 (530) 470-9280 (*www.globalfamily.net*)

We are an international network of individuals and groups who choose to experience themselves as members of one human family. Global Family promotes activities and processes that enable people to experience their deeper connection to one another, to the Earth, and to their source.

Grameen Bank, Bhaban Mirpur - 2, Dhaka -1216, Bangladesh. Tel. (880-2) 8011138 (*www.grameen-info.org*)

Founded by Mohammed Yunus. Grameen Bank has reversed conventional banking practice by removing the need for collateral and created a banking system based on mutual trust, accountability, participation, and creativity.

Green America, 1612 K Street NW, Suite 600, Washington, D.C. 20006, USA. Tel. +1 (800) 584-7336 (*www.greenamerica.org*)

Green America promotes environmental sustainability, social justice, and economic justice.

Guayakí Organic Yerba Mate, 6784 Sebastopol Ave., Sebastopol, CA 95472, USA. Tel: +1 (888) 482-9254 (*www.guayaki.com*)

A Fair-Trade Certified Company. Their mission is to steward and restore 200,000 acres of South American Atlantic rainforest and create over 1,000 living wage jobs by 2020 by leveraging a market-driven restoration business model.

Hazel Henderson, P.O Box 5190, St. Augustine, FL 32085, USA. Tel. +1 (904) 829-3140 (*www.hazelhenderson.com*)

Hazel is an author, world-renowned futurist, evolutionary economist, and worldwide syndicated columnist. Watch a video by Nathalie Beekman about her life on the website. Find out more at *www. ethicalmarkets.tv.*

Hummingbird Ranch Community, PO Box 732, Mora, New Mexico 87732, USA. (*www.hummingbirdcommunity.org*)

Nestled in a valley among the Sangre de Cristo Mountains of northern *New Mexico* is a 500-acre *ranch* that is home to the *Hummingbird* Community, a great example of co-creative living.

The Kelso Institute, USA. (*www.kelsoinstitute.org*)

Includes quotes, lectures, bibliography, book reviews, papers, and downloadable books about the political-economic ideas of Louis Kelso.

Mondragon Corporation, Pº Jose Mª Arizmendiarrieta nº 5, 20500 Mondragon–Gipuzkoa, Spain. Tel. +34 (943) 779 300 (*www.mondragon-corporation.com/language/en-US/ENG.aspx*)

Mondragon Corporation, a world leader in the cooperative movement, is the largest business group in the Basque Country and the seventh-largest in Spain.

Peace Trails, Mill Cottage Letcoombe Bassett, Wantage, Oxfordshire OX12 9LL, United Kingdom. Tel. +44 (0) 1235-760687 (*www.peace-trails.com*)

Peace Trails is the website of Gabriella Kapfer, musician and sound-weaver. Peace trails offers sound workshops for healing, journeys, retreats, etc. (Gabriella is also cofounder of CareFirstWorld Ltd.)

Public Banking Institute, USA. (*www.publicbankinginstitute.org*)

Banking in the public interest. A think-tank, research, and advisory organization disseminating information about publicly owned banks. They educate lawmakers and policy-makers so they can write and pass legislation that creates affordable credit for the very people whom they represent. An initiative of Ellen Brown, author of *Web of Debt*.

Ryan's Well Foundation, P.O. Box 1120, 215 Van Buren Street, Kemptville, Ontario, K0G 1J0, Canada. Tel. +1 (613) 258-6832 (*www.ryanswell.ca*)

The Ryan's Well Foundation is a charity committed to delivering access to safe water as an essential way to improve the lives of people in the developing world.

STWR—Share The World's Resources, P.O. Box 52662, London, N7 8UX, UK. Tel. +44 (0) 20 7609 3034 (*www.stwr.org*)

STWR advocates for essential resources such as food, water, and energy to be shared internationally under the agency of the United Nations.

SRI in the Rockies, 5475 Mark Dabling Boulevard, Suite 108, Colorado Springs, Colorado 80918 USA. Tel.+1 (888) 774-2663 (*www.sriintherockies.com*)

SRI in the Rockies is the premier annual gathering of investors and investment professionals working to direct the flow of investment capital in more positive, healthy, and transformative ways. Email: info@sriintherockies.com.

TimeBanks USA, 5500 39th St. NW, Washington, D.C. 20015, USA. Tel. +1 (202) 686-5200 (*www.timebanks.org*)

Founded by Edgar Kahn. For every hour you spend doing something for someone in your neighborhood, you earn one Time Dollar. Then you have a Time Dollar to spend on having someone do something for you. Time Banks change neighborhoods and whole communities. Time Banking is a social change movement in twenty-two countries and on six continents.

Triodos Bank, NV, Headquarters: Utrechtseweg 44, Postbus 55. 3700 AB Zeist, The Netherlands. Tel. +31 (030) 693-6500 (*www.triodos.nl*)

With banks in Belgium, Germany, Spain and United Kingdom, (*www. triodos.com*) Triodos is a bank that lends to and invests in organizations that benefit people and the environment. Voted the world's most sustainable bank in 2009.

US SIF—The Forum for Sustainable and Responsible Investment, 910 17th Street NW Suite 1000, Washington, DC 20006, USA. Tel. +1 (202) 872-5361 (*www.ussif.org*)

Formerly the Social Investment Forum (SIF). It is the U.S. membership association for professionals, firms, institutions, and organizations engaged in socially responsible and sustainable investing.

Web of Debt, by Ellen Hodgson Brown, USA. (*www.webofdebt.com*)

Web of Debt tells the shocking truth about our money system and how we can break free. All about the debt-based foundation our present financial system, and its compound interest.

Woman's Peace Collection, (*womenspeacecollection.com*)

The Women's Peace Collection is an enterprise that fully supports women in regions of conflict and post-conflict—as mothers, peace builders, entrepreneurs, and skilled artisans. To advance their mission further and more quickly, they have launched a partnership between the Amber Chand Foundation and the Women's Peace Collection (formerly The Amber Chand Collection), bridging nonprofit goals with those of a profit-making enterprise. The Amber Chand Foundation was launched in 2008 as a nonprofit grantmaking institution and is a program initiative of Trusteeship Institute, a 501(c)(3) non-profit based in western Massachusetts that supports

Gandhi's principles of stewardship for socially responsible businesses. For more information, email amber@amberchand.com or call (800) 979-0108. To learn more about their work and founder, Amber Chand, visit *amberchand.com*.

World Finance Initiative, (*www.carefirstworld.com*)

Scottish Charitable Company, founded in 1996 by Louis and Sandra Böhtlingk. We lived in Scotland till 2008, when we moved to the Netherlands. At present (July 2011) the company only has a postal address for its registered office in Scotland itself. World Finance Initiative is the parent company for both CareFirstWorld Ltd and Zorg Eerst Projecten. The best way to contact us is through our website and by e-mail: daretocare@carefirstworld.com.

Zorg Eerst Projecten (Care First Projects), Saffierstraat 35, 9743 LG, Groningen, The Netherlands. +31 (050)-573-5071 (*www.carefirstworld.com*)

This is the home address of and Martha Reijnders, who founded the charity with us (Louis and Sandra Bohtlingk) in 2002. It is the Dutch branch of World Finance Initiative. The best way to contact us through our website and our e-mail: *daretocare@carefirstworld.com*.

ABOUT THE AUTHOR

L OUIS BÖHTLINGK is a visionary who has worked as a psychic and intuitive counselor since 1981. With his wife Sandra, he has created multiple platforms with which to address the money issues that individuals and companies experience. He is the founder of the Scottish charity World Finance Initiative, the trading subsidiary of that charity, CareFirstWorld Ltd., and a Dutch branch of their work, Zorg Eerst Projecten (Care First Projects), which includes the School of Care. Recently, Louis and Sandra have also started a Care Fund (Community Care Bank), assisting individuals and businesses in need through a network where members provide money and support. Louis is also the creator of the "Meeting the Mystery of Money" workshop, which has been held throughout the United States, United Kingdom, and the Netherlands and helps individuals to reorganize their finances and lives with a care-first approach. You can learn more about the work Louis and Sandra do on their website, *www.carefirstworld.com*. Louis can be reached by email at daretocare@carefirstworld.com. Louis lives with his wife in Lelystad in the Netherlands.

COSIMO is a specialty publisher of books and publications that inspire, inform, and engage readers. Our mission is to offer unique books to niche audiences around the world.

COSIMO BOOKS publishes books and publications for innovative authors, nonprofit organizations, and businesses.

COSIMO BOOKS specializes in bringing books back into print, publishing new books quickly and effectively, and making these publications available to readers around the world.

COSIMO CLASSICS offers a collection of distinctive titles by the great authors and thinkers throughout the ages.

At **COSIMO CLASSICS** timeless works find new life as affordable books, covering a variety of subjects including: Business, Economics, History, Personal Development, Philosophy, Religion & Spirituality, and much more!

COSIMO REPORTS publishes public reports that affect your world, from global trends to the economy, and from health to geopolitics.

FOR MORE INFORMATION CONTACT US AT
INFO@COSIMOBOOKS.COM

➤ if you are a book lover interested in our current catalog of books

➤ if you represent a bookstore, book club, or anyone else interested in special discounts for bulk purchases

➤ if you are an author who wants to get published

➤ if you represent an organization or business seeking to publish books and other publications for your members, donors, or customers.

COSIMO BOOKS ARE ALWAYS
AVAILABLE AT ONLINE BOOKSTORES

VISIT COSIMOBOOKS.COM
BE INSPIRED, BE INFORMED

CPSIA information can be obtained at www.ICGtesting.com
Printed in the USA
BVOW071435311011

274894BV00005BA/1/P